D0485297

No Lasting Home

NO LASTING HOME

A Year in the Paraguayan Wilderness

EMMY BARTH

Foreword by Alfred Neufeld

THE PLOUGH PUBLISHING HOUSE

Published by The Plough Publishing House
of Church Communities Foundation, Rifton, NY 12471 USA
and by Church Communities UK
Robertsbridge, East Sussex TN32 5DR UK

Acknowledgments

Cover paintings by Victor Crawley (1899–1991). Photographs on pages 26, 40, 45, 46 are reprinted courtesy of the Mennonite Church USA Archives in North Newton, Kansas. Photographs on pages 29, 31, 33, 36, 41 are reprinted courtesy of the Mennonite Archives in Filadelfia, Paraguay. All other photographs are from the archives of the Plough Publishing House.

All diaries and letters quoted in this book are from the archives of the Plough Publishing House, unless otherwise noted, and are used with permission.

Library of Congress Cataloging-in-Publication Data

Barth, Emmy, 1961-

    No lasting home : a year in the Paraguayan wilderness / Emmy Barth ;
    foreword by Alfred Neufeld.
        p. cm.
    Includes bibliographical references.
    ISBN 978-0-87486-945-3
    1. Bruderhof Communities--Paraguay--History. I. Title.
    BX8129.B635P379 2009
    289.7'892--dc22

                                                        2009015768

Printed in the U.S.A.

*In grateful memory
of all those Paraguayan pioneers,
Bruderhof and Mennonite alike,
who left homeland and loved ones
for the sake of their faith
and laid down their lives
for us, the living.*

BRAZIL

BOLIVIA

Gran

PARAGUAY

Chaco

★Asunción

Rio de Janeiro

Rio Paraná

URUGUAY

Buenos
Aires

Montevideo

Rio de la Plata

ARGENTINA

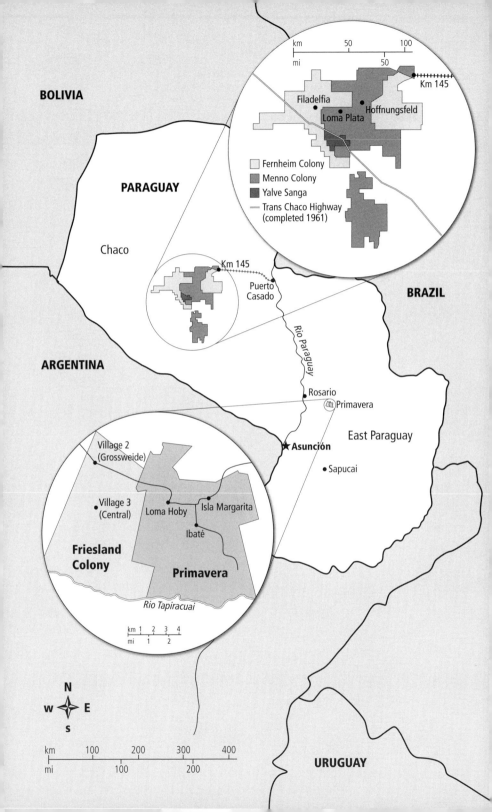

BOLIVIA

PARAGUAY

km | 50 | 100
mi | 50

Km 145

Filadelfia
Loma Plata   Hoffnungsfeld

☐ Fernheim Colony
■ Menno Colony
■ Yalve Sanga
— Trans Chaco Highway
  (completed 1961)

Chaco

Km 145

Puerto
Casado

BRAZIL

Río Paraguay

ARGENTINA

Rosario
Primavera

Asunción

East Paraguay

Sapucai

Village 2
(Grossweide)

Village 3
(Central)   Loma Hoby   Isla Margarita

Ibaté

Friesland
Colony   Primavera

Río Tapiracuai

km 1 2 3 4
mi   1   2

N
W ✦ E
S

km | 100 | 200 | 300 | 400
mi | 100 | 200

URUGUAY

THE GRAN CHACO, a region central to the telling of this story, is a grand plain west of the Paraguay River and east of the Andes. It lies mainly within Paraguay, but extends into Bolivia and Argentina as well. Roughly 250,001 mi² (647,500 km²) in size, it consists of three parts: the Alto Chaco, whose highlands meet the Andes and are extremely dry and sparsely vegetated; the Chaco Boreal to the east, with less severe aridity and higher thorn trees; and finally (moving farther to the east) the Bajo Chaco, a savanna-like territory dotted with palms, quebracho trees, and high grass.

CONTENTS

THE QUEST

To meet the challenge of the sun
Awake and gird thyself my soul,
Put forth upon the outward way
To seek the shining goal.

Go seek the land of Brotherhood,
Go seek the city on a hill,
One love shall bind thee to all those
Who seek with heart and will.

And though the sun climb up the sky,
And hot salt sweat pour down thy face,
Turn not aside, for pause or shade.
Expect no resting place.

Fear not the sun shall beat thee down,
Though heart shall faint and limbs shall fail,
But look ahead with eager eyes
The far and fiery trail.

And joyful journey on, until,
One with thy brothers in the quest,
Thou build the city on the hill
Where all shall find true rest.

PHILIP BRITTS
March 1941, mid-Atlantic

FOREWORD

WHEN MY FATHER-IN-LAW, Dr. Wilhelm Kaethler, died, he left numerous papers that needed sorting. A surgeon in Paraguay for most of his adult life, he had worked with Cyril Davies and Ruth Land – two Bruderhof physicians – in Friesland and Primavera. (His wife, my mother-in-law, Frieda Siemens, was the daughter of Nikolai Siemens, long-time editor of the *Menno-Blatt*, and a close friend of Emmy Arnold and her sons.) Among the old papers, I found an anniversary edition of *Der Pflug*, the Bruderhof quarterly, in which Emmy recalls the history of their community. Unbelievably, it had been published in Primavera. How could a publication of such quality come out of our poor country, and so long ago, I wondered?

I eagerly read through the little journal. I knew the community's history, for I had read Ulrich Egger's book, *Community for Life* (1985). But these firsthand reports by the original founders of the Bruderhof appealed far more to my emotions. Later, going to Friesland and talking with my mother-in-law, I learned many remarkable things from her memories of the *Hutterer* or *Bruderhöfler* or *Barbudos* ("bearded ones"), as they were known here during their twenty-year stay in Paraguay. It is a fascinating history, though virtually unknown by most young Mennonites of our country.

Several years later, while in Akron, Pennsylvania, mutual acquaintances at the MCC (Mennonite Central Committee) led me into direct contact with the Bruderhof by means of visits to Woodcrest and Maple Ridge, two of their communities in upstate New York. Those were unforgettable days. Here were an amazing group of people, many of them born and raised in Paraguay, and several still speaking good Spanish! One had done a nurse's training in Asunción (at the same school my wife Wilma attended). Another remembered dancing the fox trot at the Colegio Internacional. Still another reminded me of Behage, the well-known arts and crafts store in Asunción, where the community used to sell its wooden turnery and I used to go shopping. And there was *Frau Doktor* Ruth Land, now in her nineties, but still with the most vivid memories.

On another visit (this time to Sannerz, Germany, where the Bruderhof has again settled in its very first home), a member of the community showed me a copy of an old *Friedensmanifest*, or peace manifesto. Drawn up at the 1936 Mennonite World Conference in Amsterdam, this document was signed by Mennonite leaders such as Harold S. Bender, Orie Miller, C. F. Klassen, and C. N. Hiebert—and by Emmy Arnold and Hans Zumpe of the Bruderhof.* A radical condemnation of militarism and war, signed under the gathering clouds of what developed into World War II, this manifesto immediately recalled the famous Barmen Declaration of the Confessing Church of 1934, in which Karl Barth, Dietrich Bonhoeffer, and others condemned

*See Appendix 3.

the cult of the *Führer* and the secular messianism of the National Socialists.

All these threads and more have come together for me in this book, especially in the chapter "Paraguayan Nazis?" where Emmy Arnold is quoted as saying *"Lieber Haken-wurm als Hakenkreuz!"* which translates as "better hook-worm, than hooked cross (swastika)." Reading this section of the book, I remembered my own father, Peter K. Neufeld, who through the witness of Eberhard and Emmy Arnold's Bruderhof, and through the strong spiritual support of Nikolai Siemens, underwent conversion from a pro-German militant to a pointed opponent of the Nazi movement then growing in Fernheim. (Siemens and my father had been secretaries of the Unión Germanica in the Chaco, but were formally expelled because of their anti-Nazi views.) Looking back, it seems that my father might have drawn inspiration from the 1936 Amsterdam peace manifesto. Clearly, love to one's enemies and the sharing of material goods, as well as the radical discipleship of Jesus within a pilgrim church, were central pillars of his faith until the end of his life.

Emmy Barth has done a wonderful job uncovering old documents and bringing to life the Bruderhof's exodus from England and its first year in Paraguay. Among the sources she sent me while researching this book were two letters from the Bruderhof, written in England in 1940, reminding the Mennonites of the memorandum they had co-signed in Amsterdam in 1936. Not only a manifesto but a covenant of mutual help, the statement had included a promise to aid one another, if either branch of the Anabaptist family ever suffered persecution because of its commitment to the way of Jesus.

One year later, Hitler's Gestapo was to expel the Bruderhof from Germany; three years after that, now on the run from England, they were seeking refuge in South America with the help of Orie Miller and the MCC. This book relates their extraordinary story.

Alfred Neufeld
Asunción, Paraguay

1

VOYAGE

*We must be ready always to step
out into the unknown at the call of
God—as Abraham did. Let us be a
pilgrim church on the move, trusting
God to lead us where he wants.*

MAUREEN BURN

TRAUTEL GROANED and stumbled dizzily back to her
bed, fighting nausea as the ship rolled under her feet. In the
basket next to her bed, her baby stirred. Felix was only five
weeks old and had cried most of the night. He was quiet
now, but she herself could not sleep. What lay ahead for
her little one? "God, why are you leading us into the dan-
ger-ridden tropics? What sacrifices will be demanded of
us?" She remembered the fear that had clutched her heart
in Liverpool as she crossed the gangplank onto the ship,
little Felix held tight in her arms. She felt that the lives of
all of them were on a razor's edge, suspended between
life and death, heaven and earth. "Will I ever touch solid

Operated by England's famed Blue Star Line, which took passengers to and from
South America from 1927 until 1972, the Andalucia Star was torpedoed off West
Africa in 1942.

ground again? Will the demon of war let this big ship pass
unscathed?" She pulled herself together. "Do not question, my soul, but trust. God is leading us out of a war-torn
country. He will protect us and our children on the ocean
and also in the strange land we are travelling to."

It was the end of November 1940. They were on a luxury
liner, the *Andalucia Star,* one of the few passenger ships to
dare the submarine-infested ocean. It had no second-class
berths, so the eighty refugees she was travelling with had
been forced to pay for first-class tickets.

Leo and Trautel Dreher had left Switzerland eleven
years earlier to join the Bruderhof, a Christian community
then located in Germany. Little could they have known
what taking this step would mean: how they would soon
have to flee Hitler's minions for England, and then England, too, for the sake of their convictions. Now they were

Trautel Dreher (center) with Gertie Vigar (left) and a group of children in England, ca. 1940. Trautel came to the Bruderhof with her fiancé Leo in 1929.

on their way to Paraguay, that mysterious, landlocked, little country in the backwoods of South America, with six small children.

Marianne Zimmermann was on the ship too, with her husband Kurt and their four children. She kept a journal for her children to read when they grew up:

> With this voyage, a new period of our community's history begins. We've taken leave of a beautiful home and are now preparing for a new life. I would like to write something for you, my beloved children, about this trip, which will have great significance. The goal, the castle and the city in which Jesus lives, is and remains the same, even if there are many unknown paths before us. We must look unwaveringly to

Jesus; Peter was able to walk safely on the water as long as he looked to Jesus.

Phyllis Rabbitts, a young English nurse and midwife who had come to the community only a few months earlier, wrote a letter to her family describing the departure. She was to follow on a later voyage to Paraguay:

> The idea of a whole community being transferred from one country to another in wartime was something one could not grasp. It seemed too great a miracle. We had realized for many months the insecurity of our position in England as there was so much hate growing in the hearts of the general populace. This could be understood because we had many German members; also the pacifism of our English members roused a bitter spirit in nationalistic minds.
>
> Although national and local government officials were tolerant and understanding, our economic position was getting acute because of the local hostility, which crippled our business. Also the curfew affecting our "alien" members curtailed considerably our sending out brothers for mission. The church was in peril and had to be saved, and there was a definite leading from God that we should leave the country.
>
> Following this leading from God was not easy. We had a well built-up Bruderhof – the dwelling houses were still quite new, and the dining/meeting room was brand new and beautiful in its simplicity. The laundry with its modern machines had also not long been set in motion and was a tremendous boon to those who had known what it was to wash everything by hand in difficult conditions. The new baths and toilets were also a very welcome achievement. In fact, all over

the whole Bruderhof one could see the fruits of four to five years struggle and hard labor.

But now the time had come to lay down our tools and leave all this and to pick them up again in another country that we could not choose for ourselves.

Having so many young children and several elderly and infirm members, all this was far from easy, for no one could foresee this kind of journey in wartime. Twenty-two babies were born in the year 1940 (one was stillborn) and twenty in the previous year, so there were many very young children taken to Paraguay.

After a long seeking and waiting to know the will of God concerning us, the first group left the Cotswold Bruderhof to build up afresh in a hither-to unknown (to us) land – the Chaco region of Paraguay! It was with sad and heavy hearts that we saw our brothers and sisters and children depart from us just a month before Christmas 1940. Paraguay seemed such a long way off, and between there and England lay the dangerous ocean, where ships were being either sunk or bombed almost daily.

The day of departure was a memorable one. We break-fasted together in our beautiful new dining room. We talked and sang together and felt the warmth of fellowship. Soon the coaches came that were to take the first group to the [train] station. Those who could accompanied them and sang songs at the station as the train took its departure. Would we ever see them again? How long would it be until we were all reunited once more? For what purpose were we being led out of England to Paraguay? Many such questions filled our thoughts. But deep down in our hearts was a strong feeling that ere long this reunion would come and together we would

Departure from the Cotswold Bruderhof, Ashton-Keynes, England, November 1940.

continue the fight and struggle so that God's will might be done through us, wherever that might be.

The going away of this first large group left a big gap in our midst, and we longed increasingly for reunion. Yet if it were not to be, we were prepared to remain where we were and carry on the witness of a life of brotherhood – even to death.

On board the *Andalucia Star* the passengers found their cabins and settled in. The voyage would take several weeks. Already the first evening several were seasick and did not make it to dinner. The next morning hardly anyone was able to get up. Most of the children were sick, and big strong men had to be encouraged to come up onto the deck, where they lay on deck chairs, white as chalk. Emmy, the eldest in the group, encouraged the men to rise to the adventure. Though fighting seasickness herself, she roused them:

Emmy Arnold (1884–1980), widow of Eberhard Arnold and co-founder of the Bruderhof, at the Cotswold Bruderhof shortly before the voyage.

"Come on! Get up and take a little walk. We are pioneers!"

Emmy was *Mama* to many of the adults and *Oma* (grand-mother) to all the children. It was she and her late husband, Eberhard Arnold, who had initially formed the community now known as the Bruderhof in a small village in Germany, in 1920. Amid the economic and political rubble left by the nation's crushing defeat in World War I, they had turned their backs on middle-class life and sought to take liter-ally Jesus' demands in the Sermon on the Mount. Within months, they had been joined by other like-minded seekers from across Europe and from many walks of life. Seventeen years later, in 1937, the community had been forced out of Germany. As Nazi records explain, the community's very existence was a threat since it "represents a world view totally opposed to National Socialism. Its members reject the race laws…and oppose the institutions of the Third Reich." After surrounding the community's farm and imprisoning its leaders (mercifully, all were later released), the Nazis gave them forty-eight hours to leave the country. The community fled to England by way of Holland. Now they had been uprooted once more.

With her sense of humor and a solid, simple faith, Emmy encouraged distraught mothers, too: "Come, let's walk around the deck," and started singing an old hiking song, "We want to travel round the globe just like Columbus did, for people are so very dull in this, our latitude!"

Every meal was served in the ship's five-star restaurant. Many of the group had never eaten in such a grand style. What should they order from the fancy menu, and would the children eat it anyway? Which knife should be used for what? A four-year-old, Johannes, tried to eat with three forks at once; and Trautel's son, Josua, spilled his milk on the carpet. She found herself longing for a simple stew.

The ship seemed to be travelling north, although no one spoke about the route it was taking, for reasons of security. The weather was cold and stormy—chairs fell over, and dishes slid off the tables. A child fell out of his bunk and bumped his forehead. Emmy's daughter-in-law Edith (she

Edith Boecker Arnold (shown here with her daughter Mirjam on the deck of the Andalucia Star) left her studies at Tübingen to join the Bruderhof in 1932; she married Hardy Arnold, a fellow student, soon afterward.

was married to Hardy Arnold) fell over backward while feeding her daughter Mirjam.

Five days into the crossing, Edith, who had been feeling sick, suffered a miscarriage. Heavy-hearted – not only over her own loss, but on account of the other young mothers who had little ones or were expecting babies – she turned her thoughts to God and reminded herself why they were here: they were on a quest for peace, justice, and community and could not let the hardships of war obstruct their path. Writing later to the remnant of the community that had stayed behind in England, she explained:

> I have the feeling that our church will be faced with a struggle
> for faith in the near future. The powers of evil are especially

active just now; they will not suffer the arising of a Zion, of a city of peace. The powers of evil will attack us in different ways in Paraguay than in England, but it is the same fight. Yet wherever the kingdom of God is revealed, demons yield! We need the power of a faith that is completely different from pious feeling. The faith that is required of us does not come from our own strength — our own strength is even a hindrance to faith. We cannot overcome evil; we are too weak. Only God can do this.

The First of Advent (four Sundays before Christmas), traditionally marks the beginning of the holiday season in Germany, and the Bruderhof group made the most of it. After breakfast in the ship's dining room, they gathered in the salon. To everyone's surprise, several sisters had decorated it with evergreen branches and a wreath they had brought with them from England. As each child was given a candle to light, the group broke into songs, Margrit accompanying them on her violin. In the evening the adults met again. Emmy's son, Hardy, read from the Gospel of Luke, carols were sung, and punch was passed around.

While such gatherings for celebration and worship strengthened and united the group, they were almost always accompanied by reminders of the very different atmosphere surrounding them. On this occasion, for example, curious passengers kept peeping in at them through the windows of the smoking room. Further, the general mood on the ship was most depressing: passengers and crew were very much aware of the danger of submarines and warships and, for the first few days, danger from airplanes. Defense guns and three machine guns were constantly manned, and blackout precautions strictly observed. To avoid being followed, the ship's course was changed constantly and without warning. For the first week everyone had to carry life belts at all times. Every three or four days there was a lifeboat drill. Each of the community's children was paired with an adult who was to make sure they got in the lifeboats. Each child also wore an ID card around his or her neck in case of separation from their parents.

On the whole, the ship's crew and stewards were friendly, especially to the children. For the adults, getting to know their fellow passengers was a little more difficult, if only because of language barriers. There were Jewish refugees from Poland, Russia, Czechoslovakia, and Germany, as well as political refugees from France and England. A few connections were established: Hardy struck up a friendship with an Argentinean banker and his wife, who were particularly concerned that the children get good milk and food once in Paraguay and advised them to take a few cows upriver. A Brazilian diplomat suggested that Brazil would be more favorable than Paraguay and offered to write a letter of recommendation to the immigration department. The ship's doctor, a jovial and easy-going man, offered the travelers lectures on tropical diseases and hygiene.

One thing everyone seemed to enjoy was the community's singing—whether it was Christmas carols or folk songs to cheer up those who were seasick. Singing had always been an integral part of the community life, and at sea this was all the more the case.

Bruderhof passengers on the Andalucia Star's dangerous transatlantic crossing fought cabin fever and fear by folk dancing on the deck.

Occupying the children—and keeping them away from the railings—was a full-time job, and because ping pong and other such activities were difficult to play on the rolling ship, playtime songs and circle games were popular.

Several of the group took up studying Spanish. Meanwhile, small knots of brothers dreamed of the building up that lay ahead. Planning a school, a kitchen, workshops, and gardens, they discussed everything from potential sources of income to how they might reestablish a publishing house.

The weather was growing warmer as the ship headed south. The sickle moon was now a cradle in the sky, no longer upright. It was strange to see new stars. Had they crossed the equator? Large flocks of white birds skimmed the water – then swooped, plunging into the ocean. (They weren't birds at all, the passengers soon realized, but flying fish.)

One night the group gave a Christmas concert for the other passengers. They had worked hard for days, rehearsing German and English carols. Margrit, Jan, and Marianne even played a violin trio. It felt a little awkward, singing about a poor baby in a manger to an audience sitting in soft armchairs, in formal evening dress, smoking cigarettes. But the audience enjoyed the music and afterwards seemed friendlier.

Now the heat became oppressive. Lightweight, light-colored pants were being sold on the ship, so a pair was bought for each of the men. On the deck, two playpens were set up in the shade for the youngest children, and the babies' bassinets were lined up next to them. Some families even began sleeping on the deck, which was cooler than the cabins. It was a beautiful way to fall asleep, too, with stars and moon twinkling above the watery expanse and the black smokestack of the ship standing out against the magnificent night sky.

On December 12 land was sighted. Far on the horizon, the mountains of Rio de Janeiro were visible. Everyone rushed to the deck. As they entered the bay, they saw beautiful green slopes on either side, covered with palms and yellow mimosa. The *Andalucia Star* anchored two or three miles out. Policemen and customs officers came out in small boats and boarded the ship. Here was a chance to send mail to the beloved ones left in England. And there was a letter from Hans Meier!

Hans had left England the previous August with Guy Johnson, a young lawyer who had recently joined the community. At a time when the Luftwaffe was raining bombs on London and Coventry, the very existence of the Bruderhof in England was increasingly viewed as a security risk, and so the two brothers had been sent to New York to research possibilities for emigration. There, with the help of sympathetic Quakers, Mennonites, South Dakota Hutterites (and a handful of notable individuals, including Eleanor Roosevelt), they sought in vain for asylum in the United States or Canada. They also inquired at numerous other embassies, including those of New Zealand, Australia, South Africa, and Jamaica. But with all of Europe at war, and North America on the brink of it, no one wanted to touch a multi-national group – especially not a counter-cultural one with strong pacifist leanings. In desperation, the two men had turned to the Mennonites, a Christian group of similar heritage and beliefs. In 1936, members of the Bruderhof had joined the Mennonite World Conference in Holland, and had co-signed a statement affirming their nonresistant position and a promise of mutual help. Orie Miller, then executive secretary of the Mennonite Central Committee (MCC), had helped Mennonite refugees from Russia and was willing to help the Bruderhof

Bruderhof member Hans Meier, a Swiss engineer, was briefly imprisoned by the Nazis in 1937. In August 1940 (the date of this picture) the community sent him to New York to research the possibility of emigration from Europe.

group too. He acted quickly, speaking directly with the Paraguayan embassy in Washington. Before long, the Bruderhof was granted permission to enter Paraguay with the same privileges given to the Mennonites: freedom of religion, freedom to run their own schools, and exemption from military service. MCC would help them find land and provide initial financial support.

Now Hans's letter was read aloud. To the great joy of the assembled passengers, which included both his and Guy's wives, the two brothers had already made it to South

America and were working out the last obstacles to immigration for the arriving group. Guy would meet them here in Rio, and Hans in Buenos Aires.

2

UP THE RIVER

*God bless the wanderers, they that
seek and seldom find — and yet all
ceaselessly do seek some truer, better
thing, some fairer country. These are
they, O Lord, who open up the hidden
ways of earth and men: for the way of
the wanderer is wide and winding, his
soul hungers after God — always are
his paths weary and without end. Yet
we feel his kinship to us all, we glory in
his findings, we enter into his heritage.
God save his soul tonight wherever he
may be and give our yearning following spirits peace.*

W. E. B. DU BOIS

THE ANDALUCIA STAR steamed down the South
American coast, stopping now and then at various ports,
until it entered the Rio de la Plata, the widest estuary in the
world, which is formed by the Uruguay and Parana Rivers.

Here at Buenos Aires Hans Meier was to meet them, and the next lap of the journey would begin. Margrit's eyes ached from straining to see him. Yes, there he was! After a lengthy discussion the ship officials finally allowed him on board, where tears of relief mingled with laughter. Here, beyond the rumble of war, husband and wife were finally together again, and both alive and well.

A doctor boarded and examined everyone. Although some of the children had a rash, he was not particularly concerned. They had to wait three days, and then the group finally, on December 21, left the luxurious ocean liner that had been their home for four weeks. They were taken by bus, under police supervision, to another part of the port, where they boarded a steamboat that was to take them up the Parana River, deep into the unknown tropics.

From now on there were no more first-class comforts. They were travelling third class, all eighty-one of them, in one large room in the hold of the ship, with no windows. There were only forty beds, so each adult shared a bed with a child. The heat was intense, the stench terrible, and the cabin dirty. Some of the women hardly dared eat the food, and Cyril Davies, the community's doctor, forbade drinking without boiling the water first. During the day they sat among the bags and trunks, trying to distract the children with songs and games. Marianne wrote:

> Now we were really entering the unknown! In spite of the terrible heat, in spite of the cramped quarters and dirt and loudly screaming Spaniards, we felt more comfortable, more that we were "on the road," on the path of the pioneers. For

The riverboat on the Rio Paraguay. Alan Stevenson is holding his hat; Kurt Zimmermann is next to him.

young people without children, the whole trip would have been an adventure. But to care for our little children was not easy, especially regarding hygiene. We bathed them in barrels that were filled with river water and in which we also washed our laundry. Many children got heat rash or other rashes.

Darkness fell quickly after the sun set, and the stars were clear and bright. The familiar constellations were upside down, and new constellations appeared. They sang Christmas carols and ate the last Christmas cookies Alfred had packed. Susi Fros, whose baby was almost due, thought of Mary: she too had traveled into the unknown; her baby too had had no home and nowhere to lay his head.

It was Christmas Day when the steamer arrived in Asunción, the Paraguayan capitol. Paraiso trees were in bloom along the streets. A woman in ragged clothes with an open black umbrella rode idly by on a donkey. The heat was oppressive. They changed boats again, getting into a small barge. First the luggage was transferred—all twenty-three tons. After that, there was no room left; the people sat squashed between their bags. The children were crying; several had fevers. Again they were to sleep in the windowless hold, but this time they got several first-class cabins for the sick and the pregnant women. Everything was very dirty, especially the water. They did not dare to wash the children in it, let alone drink it. The boat had only a canvas cover, under which they had to wait for two and a half days. They ate bananas and pineapples; other food was hard to procure. But the thirst and the heat! The children spent most of the day bathing in wooden tubs. A few young adults jumped into the river to cool off, but when a sailor shouted *"Piranha!"* they got out just as quickly. (Notoriously ferocious, these fish can smell blood, and it is said they can eat a cow down to the skeleton within minutes.)

Once more they set out, deeper and deeper into the heart of South America. They watched the riverbanks closely, trying to envision these exotic surroundings as their new home. It was hard. They chugged past mile after mile of uncultivated land, shrubs, and palm trees. Dark herons and snowy egrets stood amid the marsh grasses. Flocks of parrots and even a few toucans flew overhead. One day the children crowded to the rail to see a crocodile. A hot wind

Mothers on the riverboat endured heat, humidity, and crowding–and the
constant nagging of restless children everywhere: "How long till we get there?"
The women (L to R) are Nellie Stevenson, Sekunda Kleiner (in bonnet), and
Edith Arnold.

blew in from the shore, laden with the scent of orange blossoms. Sometimes the boat docked at small port towns, and
Paraguayans and indigenous women could be seen, carrying large baskets of bananas or *chipa*, a local bread, on their
heads.

The boat remained crowded as it went upriver, and it
was impossible to keep things orderly or clean. By now
everyone in the group truly felt like a refugee. After two
days' travel they arrived in Puerto Casado. Now, at last,
they thought, they were nearing the end of their journey.

Situated on the west bank of the Paraguay River, 190
miles north of Asunción, Puerto Casado (Puerto la Espe-

Fritz Kleiner, the community's blacksmith and building foreman, braids his daughter Traindel's hair as they make their way upriver.

ranza), was the center of a large tannery and cattle ranch, owned by the Carlos Casado Company of Buenos Aires. The company had built a narrow-gauge railroad into the interior to facilitate the shipment of quebracho logs, from which it extracted tannin.

The first group of Mennonites had arrived here in 1927, having left Canada because the Canadian government withdrew their right to conduct their schools in German. The Paraguayan government was eager to settle the inhospitable Chaco – not least, because neighboring Bolivia also laid claim to the region. Paraguay promised the Mennonites certain privileges, including exemption from military service and the right to educate their children as they pleased. But in Puerto Casado the Mennonites learned that the land they expected to purchase had not yet been surveyed. They camped in barracks and tents for sixteen months until they could proceed to their "promised land." Meanwhile many grew discouraged and returned to Canada. A typhoid epidemic broke out, and more than a hundred of those who stayed died.

The newcomers from England, of course, knew nothing of these hardships of their predecessors, nor could they have anticipated the sacrifices that their own quest to settle this harsh land would demand. They arrived around noon, the hottest time of day. The women and children arranged themselves in the shade of the jetty, while the men unloaded the crates. Soon water was boiling in large cauldrons. Half an ox, rice, and *galletas* (hard dried rolls) had been placed at their disposal.

As the women rested, there was a sudden cry – a tarantula had scuttled out from under a crate. Mosquitoes soon proved to be a bigger problem. They managed to get under the most expertly hung mosquito nets, and the constant swatting unnerved the exhausted travelers. It was a restless night; the children crying and waking those who had finally fallen asleep. Mothers lay awake, their heads swimming with new challenges. Marianne, for example, had found that all three of her young daughters had contracted lice on the

Kurt and Marianne Zimmermann, a school teacher, with their children, ca. 1941.

riverboat. She withdrew with them into a corner and began combing out their hair. "At least we are here together, alive and healthy," she comforted herself in her diary.

At five thirty the next morning they boarded the small train that was to take them into the Chaco. The train was fueled by logs and had to stop every so often to reload a supply of timber. It had no springs and swayed and jolted slowly down the track. Baby Felix fell asleep to the rocking motion. As Trautel nestled him, she looked eagerly out of the windows, trying to take in the strange, new landscape. She was dismayed. The land was flat and barren: "Is there nothing to delight our eyes, hungry as we are for beauty?

Nothing at all? There is scarcely a palm tree to be seen, not a flowery meadow, no green hills, nothing. The endless Chaco—no wonder it is known as the Green Hell! A feeling of horror grips my heart."

The journey dragged on all day. Alfred Gneiting was responsible to provide food. He managed to make coffee on a Primus stove, and some of the men passed it around, jumping from car to car.

Edith wrote: "We journeyed on and on through continuous bush, through cactus, unfamiliar trees and shrubs. Only at the beginning of our train ride did we see some lovely flowers. Every now and then, at the so-called stations, we saw straw-roofed huts. Indians came out, full of curiosity, in ragged civilian clothes, or only half dressed with sackcloth around their waists, which looked much better. Green, green, and again green—an endless wilderness passed by, with strange birds. Unredeemed nature—one felt that strongly—a wilderness that could make one melancholic."

In the evening the little train finally shuddered to a stop. The name of the terminus was as uninspired as the landscape around them, "Kilometer 145." There was a shed and a small house, where a family named the Troxlers lived. Once again there was food awaiting the exhausted group: beef, rice, and *galletas*. Mothers did what they could to bathe their tired children, wash diapers and other laundry, and arrange sleeping quarters. As the adults gathered for a simple evening meal, they raised a song of thanksgiving that they had been brought safely thus far.

The railroad from Puerto Casado was the primary means of travel to the Mennonite colonies of the Chaco Boreal.

As for the next and last lap of the journey, they were to be taken by Mennonite wagoners, but because of the Christmas holidays, Mr. Troxler told them, they might have a long wait. Wearily, they settled down for the night.

3

MENNONITES IN THE CHACO

If there were water
And no rock
If there were rock
And also water
And water
A spring
A pool among the rock
If there were the sound of water only
Not the cicada
And dry grass singing
But sound of water over a rock
Where the hermit-thrush sings
    in the pine trees
Drip drop drip drop drop drop drop
But there is no water

T. S. ELIOT

THE MENNONITES of the Chaco came in several
waves during the 1920s and 1930s and represented two different strains of the same Anabaptist stock. The inhabit-

ants of Menno Colony were Canadian émigrés fleeing anti-German sentiment after World War I. Those in the neighboring colony of Fernheim—a cluster of seventeen villages with a central settlement, Filadelfia—came from Russia, seeking refuge from Bolshevik persecution and, later, Stalinist terror.

Not surprisingly, the settlers found the vast, scrubby wasteland anything but welcoming. Like the Bruderhof refugees who followed them, they probably envisioned a subtropical paradise, only to find themselves trapped in a barren wilderness with sweltering temperatures and yearly droughts. Still, as mentioned in the previous chapter, they had been granted broad religious freedoms, and were welcomed by the Paraguayan government, which was eager to populate the region. It was these freedoms that caught the attention of the Bruderhof—an island of German speakers stranded in England at the height of the Battle of Britain.

The Bruderhof group considered themselves spiritual cousins to the Mennonites. Not only linked by similar values, they also had a formal connection with modern Anabaptism: in 1930, their founder, Eberhard Arnold, had been accepted by the Hutterites, a communal branch of Anabaptists who shared the same 16th-century German roots as the Mennonites. Luckily for the Bruderhof, MCC had a mutual regard for this affinity. In September 1940, Orie Miller responded to the pleas of Hans Meier and Guy Johnson and obtained permission for the Bruderhof to immigrate to Paraguay. He enlisted the help of the Mennonites already in the Chaco. To quote from a letter he wrote

Orie Miller and Jacob Siemens, administrators of the Mennonite Central Committee, in front of the community center in Filadelfia, 1937.

to Jacob Siemens, the MCC representative in Paraguay:

> You have no doubt heard of the small Hutterite group in England, which formerly lived in Germany and Liechtenstein and were helped to England about five years ago by the Holland Mennonites and the English Friends. They are a nonresistant group who live in two communities in England and now number about 300, about 140 adults and 160 children. A delegation composed of two of their number arrived here some weeks ago to seek opportunity for the group to migrate either to Canada or the United States. Although the group has permission to leave England and passage can be arranged, it is not possible to arrange for their migration to either of these two countries. The group has therefore decided to accept our help in going to Paraguay for settlement in

the Chaco...The Mennonite Central Committee is arranging to serve them in every way we can and has offered that they can settle on Corporación Paraguay land such as they would choose, and any not now spoken for by either Fernheim or Menno, and on the same terms that Fernheim got. They are also to be given the same help in regard to equipment and initial support as was given to our own Fernheim folks. Their US and Canada groups will arrange to finance this with our Committee. We, however, expect you to help their leaders in getting what they need and in helping them get started, and to send us charges for the same.[1]

Siemens spoke with Julius Legiehn, the *Oberschulze* (mayor) of Fernheim, and they agreed to accommodate the refugees temporarily in Filadelfia. Siemens, who had led his flock from Russia to Paraguay via China, fell sick, probably of exhaustion, in December and died on the 28th. The next day, word came that the Bruderhof group was arriving. Legiehn reported to the MCC in America:

On the morning of December 29 we buried Brother J. Siemens, and in the afternoon of the same day a telegram arrived saying that the group of Hutterites would arrive at Km 145 on Tuesday, December 31, and that we should have forty wagons there to meet them. That evening we received an airmail letter from Hans Meier saying that the group consisted of eighty-one persons and that they had twenty-three tons of equipment. I was not completely informed as to this immigration as Brother Siemens had been seeing to all the arrangements. But since there was no time to lose, I immediately called my fellow officers together and we decided that

The Troxler family home at Km 145 – a landmark, and a welcome place of rest in an otherwise desolate part of the Chaco.

the head of the colony, that is, the *Oberschulze*, should take over the MCC service until MCC told us otherwise. In the evening of December 29 we sent twenty-two wagons to Km 145, and sixteen more followed the next morning.[2]

-+->-<-+-

As the sky grew light at Km 145, the camp slowly came to life. Mothers nursed their babies and helped the older children find their clothes; fathers built up the fire and put on water to boil for coffee. Here and there, a child could be heard crying.

"The Mennonites will be coming," Mr. Troxler told them when they inquired about the next leg of the journey, "but you may have to wait a few days. It's Christmas, after all." They stared, unbelieving at the desolate landscape

around them. They had come all the way from Europe for
this? They had already been on the road for weeks, and apparently there was plenty of travelling ahead, before they
would reach what was to be their new home.

Then, in a cloud of dust across the camp (as the Paraguayan prairie was called), they saw a procession of horse
wagons coming down the road. The Mennonites were
arriving. Several men jumped down, their clothes flop-
ping loosely, their feet bare or in rough sandals. They had
come to transport the group to their village. It would take
two nights and a day to get there, and as the best times to
travel were twilight and dawn (the coolest times of day),
they had better get going immediately. Soon the women
were preparing a lunch from the beef and rice left from
the night before, and the men were loading the most necessary luggage.

Around four in the afternoon everyone piled onto the
wagons, wedging themselves between, or on top of, their
bags and cases. Hans Meier and Fritz Kleiner went ahead to
make arrangements for the group at their destination. Alan
Stevenson, Rudi Hildel, and Hans Grimm stayed behind
with the freight; additional wagons were to bring them
later. Pregnant mothers were put in the first wagon, where
the dust would be less.

The road was simply a sandy wagon track through
the undergrowth, and because the wagons had no seats
or springs, they bumped over every pothole, jolting the
passengers. Overhanging tree branches and thorn bushes
brushed their faces, and red-brown dust filled their noses

Mennonite wagons were used to transport all freight between Km 145 and Filadelfia.

and eyes. Marianne looked in amazement at the red and yellow blossoms of the smaller cactuses and at the huge cactus trees. Every growing thing seemed to have thorns or prickles. She told her children one story after another, while Emmy kept singing hiking songs.

One of the young Mennonite drivers had such painful eyes that he could not drive his wagon, so Tommy took over. It was by now so dark that they could not see the road, but the sturdy little horse felt her way along and padded after the others. This was their first encounter with the eye troubles that so many of the Mennonite children suffered from.

They did not stop for supper. Alfred and John, a young English brother, ran to the front of the wagon train with a load of *galletas* and corned beef, which they handed out as the wagons passed. Watermelons that the Mennonites

Mud, heat, insects, and deep ruts made travel a nightmare—or an adventure.

had brought along—a fruit the Europeans had never tasted but savored in the oppressive heat—were passed around as well. Fireflies flitted, and the stars seemed close enough to touch. Just before midnight the drivers called a halt. It was the last day of 1940. They lit a bonfire and sang to welcome in the New Year, remembering as they did so their brothers and sisters in England. Hardy then led them in prayer, giving thanks for God's protection over them thus far and asking for his continued guidance in the new year. Then they lay down on blankets under the open sky. Orion flickered above them, upside down, and the Southern Cross was just rising. Strange frogs croaked and insects chirped.

It was a short night. Before dawn, they set out again to make use of the coolest time of day. On and on they drove, farther and farther from civilization. "We'll reach the moon yet!" Fritz called out. "Oh no," Adolf responded, "we passed it long ago." Occasionally they caught a glimpse of indigenous people in the undergrowth, but they met no one on the road.

Shortly before noon they arrived at Hoffnungsfeld ("field of hope"). Here there was a large shed where they could relax during the hottest hours. By now several of the children were crying, their tears streaking their dusty faces. Susi remembered: "Although the place was called 'field of hope,' my hope had evaporated. My baby was due, but this was no place to bring a child into the world. As I climbed off the wagon, thorns ripped my skirt and scratched my arms and legs. I was worn out, and when I lay down on my blanket, I could not stop the tears. Just then someone walked by and wordlessly laid a bar of chocolate next to me – dear brother Adolf." Brown water from a lagoon was boiled – ten minutes, to kill the germs, at Cyril's orders – and then cooled for the children. The adults made coffee, which they drank black. The Mennonite drivers told stories of their first years in the Chaco – of drought, sandstorms, mosquitoes, and stinging flies; and of the snakebites, malaria, and typhoid that took so many lives. Trautel listened apprehensively, her heart heavy with foreboding.

While the others rested, Fritz Kleiner studied the construction of the shed. He and the other brothers were constantly thinking about the daunting task of building

Ruts were all that marked the main road into Filadelfia.

shelters for three hundred people. This was a simple struc-
ture, a roof mounted on posts. Something similar would
serve until proper houses could be built. Fritz pulled out
his notebook and his tape measure. He tested the wood and
examined the grass-covered roof.

In mid afternoon, the journey continued until it was too
dark to see the road ahead. Then supper was prepared:
black coffee, again, and *galletas*. A short night, and they
were off once more. Toward morning the first Mennonite
houses appeared, friendly and inviting, whitewashed clay
and brick houses with straw roofs. In the morning of January 2, 1941, at seven, they drove up the wide, dusty road
into Filadelfia.

School desks had been brought outside and bowls of water set on them, and the travelers were invited to wash off
the dust of the long journey. After this they were led to the

verandah of the *Gemeindehaus* (community center) where long tables had been laid with white cloths and a delicious breakfast: bread and butter, cheese, eggs, jam, fruit, coffee, milk, and sugar.

Remarkable people they are, Trautel thought to herself, noting their work-worn bodies and battle-weary, almost bitter faces. "You poor, courageous people – how much you have had to endure already! Will we soon look like that too?"

A description of their arrival appeared in *Menno-Blatt*, the Fernheim newspaper, written by its editor Nicolai Siemens:

> The Hutterites are here! After dawn the wagons with their dust-laden passengers rolled up to the main colony building. The people, though they were surely quite tired, looked pleased and cheerful, and many a warm handshake was exchanged between us.
>
> An amazing reunion! Members of these communities, closely related to us from Reformation times: on the one hand spiritual descendants of Jakob Hutter, that courageous Tyrolean of the Moravian Anabaptist movement, and on the other hand spiritual children of the East Friesian Menno Simons – both of whom dared to protest four hundred years ago against the secularization of the church – find one another again after various wanderings through the world. Suffering and persecution, war and revolution have not been able to extinguish their faith. Bolshevik terror in Russia and recent massacres in Europe have brought them together again here in the distant Chaco (practically "behind the moon," in the humorous phrase of one of their leaders). Now they are

face to face, having known of one another only from books before. *They,* bearded, upright men wearing knee-length trousers and vests, looking typically "Anabaptist" such as one finds on old pictures, their women in long, pleated skirts and center-parted hair with wonderful bonnets; *we* wearing more modern clothing but bearing the unmistakable mark of the tropics, tanned skin.

We are amazed about the fresh and joyful spirit of our guests; they all laugh and chat away so happily. And then the group of lively children! You have to see it to believe it.

After washing off the worst of the dust, all of them mixed up together sat down to the laid tables. They sang heartily and in harmony the chorale, "Now thank we all our God," and then fell to.

On Sunday, January 4, the official welcome of the group took place in Filadelfia by the *Oberschulze,* Pastors Wiebe, Harder, and Balzer from among us, and by Hardy Arnold, the minister of their group. That evening we were able to sing many songs together, and it was noticeable that our tempo is significantly slower than that of the Hutterian community. May our encounter be a blessing for us on both sides and develop to the honor of God! [3]

4

PARAGUAYAN NAZIS?

The Nazi swastika is not a static symbol. It has motion; it is moving in a definite direction. And it is going in the absolute opposite direction of the cross.

EBERHARD ARNOLD, 1933

THE MENNONITES of Fernheim had eagerly followed events in Germany over the previous decade. They saw in Hitler hope for a new Germany to which they might some day return. Wasn't he fighting Bolshevism and promoting Christian values? In May 1933 they wrote a letter to the new German government:

> With greatest excitement we German Mennonites of the Paraguayan Chaco follow the events in our beloved Motherland and experience in spirit the national revolution of the German people. We are happy that in Germany, after a long time, a government that freely and openly professes God as Creator stands at the head of the nation...With special sympathy we hear that the current government takes seriously the realiza-

The first floor of the community center in Filadelfia, shown here in 1939, was made available to the Bruderhof group for meals and meetings. Upstairs were administrative offices and a post office.

tion of Christian principles in social, economic, and cultural life and especially emphasizes the protection of the family.[4]

In particular, the school teachers Fritz Kliewer and Julius Legiehn promoted Germany's cultural heritage in the curricula they used with the colony's youth. In 1934, Fernheim had sent Kliewer to Germany to pursue his doctorate in teaching. Swept up by the nationalistic fervor he felt there, he had written home to Legiehn:

> If one lives through such weeks in Germany, one is drawn involuntarily under the spell of the *Führer* and can do nothing else than confess oneself a National Socialist.[5]

In June 1939 Kliewer returned with his new wife, Margarete, a youth leader he had met in Berlin. Years earlier, as a young

Fritz and Margarete Kliewer, Mennonite youth leaders and teachers in the Chaco. Margarete, a German, knew Emmy Arnold from the 1920s and had visited Sannerz, the first Bruderhof. She died of typhoid fever in 1943.

woman, she had met Eberhard and Emmy Arnold and had even visited their fledgling commune, Sannerz, in 1923. She loved the simple life of the German Youth Movement, the folk songs and dances, the striving of its adherents for genuineness, for closeness to the earth, and harmony with nature.

To Emmy and her fellow members at the Bruderhof, this movement was as good as dead: as they saw it, Hitler had perverted the best ideals of the era and brainwashed Germany's youth. Even the innocent term *völkisch* had been twisted. Though it had originally referred simply to the origins of German culture – as in "folk song" or "folk dance" – it had now been distorted to reflect a nationalistic pride and entailed the outright despising of other races and cultures.

To Fritz and Margarete and their young admirers, on the other hand, the dark side of National Socialism didn't seem to exist. They saw only that Hitler was creating jobs, pulling Germany out of an economic depression, and fighting Communism. Inspired to revive German culture among their fellow believers, they set to work.

Margarete was shocked by the poverty she found in the Chaco. Many of the mothers had large families. Homes had dirt floors, and there was no way to keep out the dust. Temperatures were often over 100 degrees Fahrenheit; water was scarce; the hot, dry north wind was known to drive people to insanity. The heat seemed to drain people of energy and hope. At least a third of Fernheim's residents had given up in 1937 and moved four hundred kilometers to the southeast, to start Friesland, a new colony in a more hospitable environment.

Fritz and Margarete landed among the discouraged remnant with determination and enthusiasm. They led conferences for the local teachers, and Margarete opened a series of educational courses for the mothers. In 1939, they instituted a sports program and showed off their students' achievements in a special year-end performance, marching to the music of the Kliewers' gramophone. At Christmas, they set up a tree and presented the community with a selection of German Christmas carols.

The children loved their new teachers, as did *Oberschulze* Legiehn. But others had reservations. Girls dancing and performing gymnastics in public? Marching to militaristic music? Traditionally, the Mennonites had been a "peace church," and though few of their brethren in Germany still held to this tenet (many had served in the army in World War I), most of them still did profess nonviolent resistance.

After September 1939, as they huddled around the radio in Filadelfia to follow the unfolding of a dramatic new war

in Europe, it was clear where their sympathies lay. Many
hoped that if Germany was victorious over Russia, they
might be able to leave the desolation of the Chaco and return. True, it would mean compulsory military service, but
that no longer seemed so bad. Fritz and Margarete found
themselves at the center of a battleground between a nationalistic *völkisch* group and a more conservative "pacifist" group. When school opened again after the summer
holidays in 1940, several parents kept their children home.[6]

It was into this tension that the Bruderhof group un-
wittingly arrived in January 1941. Margarete Kliewer was
excited to recognize Emmy Arnold. Although many years
had passed, both women had retained something from the
German Youth Movement: a joyful, positive attitude to life
and a sense of adventure. Together they sang the old German songs. Emmy was sympathetic to Margarete's attempts
to bring something new to the children, yet perplexed by
her political views. Hadn't the Bruderhof seen, early on,
the inherent dangers of the National Socialist agenda, and
spoken out against them, and were exiled for it?

At the same time, their common bonds allowed for sin-
cere dialogue and even a friendship of sorts. A year later,
in early 1942, Fritz and Margarete Kliewer were to visit
Emmy at Primavera, the Bruderhof's new settlement in
eastern Paraguay. Margarete died of typhoid fever the following year. Hans Boller wrote to Fritz after her death:
"When we were together last year, we sensed in your wife
a deep longing for the final kingdom of justice. We hope
you can soon visit us again and that, in the light of eternity,

we can again consider life's important questions." The whole brotherhood signed a greeting with the words, "He who believes in Jesus will live, even though he die."[7]

◂◂-▸▸

It was summer and vacation time, so the group was given ten rooms in the central schoolhouse in Filadelfia. The rooms were small and had to be shared by two families, but they were nonetheless thankful for the generosity of the Mennonites. They were also given use of the colony center, which they used as a dining and meeting room.

The air was full of swarms of tiny flies that settled on their faces and crawled into their eyes. "Is it always like this here?" Emmy asked a friendly Mennonite mother.

"Well," she answered resignedly, "As soon as they're gone, something else comes!"

At the welcome evening, Hardy told their hosts about the group's origins, of how and why they had left Europe, and of their journey. Edith wrote:

> We saw signs of much suffering in our listeners—pale, yellowish, haggard faces, miserable, tired children. We also felt a certain expectation and movement of hearts. But as we found out later, the Mennonites of the Chaco have come inwardly to an impasse. National Socialism has penetrated into the deepest wilderness and acquired many followers… though many also struggle earnestly for Christian truth. The question arose among them, "How can following Jesus and

Hitler go together?"—especially if one considers the matter of military service. They have reached a standstill and agreed not to discuss this question in the open, so as not to disturb their life together. But our coming is stirring up all these unresolved questions again.

Seventeen-year-old Elfriede Braun quickly made friends with the Mennonite young people. One evening she went home with Julius Legiehn's daughters, where one of the young men tried to convince her of the good Hitler was doing for Germany. She argued with him and told him of his oppression of the Jews. "That's just foreign propaganda," he said. "It's not true."

Every Thursday the Bruderhof group hosted an open evening. These meetings were eagerly attended; some

School buildings in Filadelfia, 1939. Note the window screens (but no glass panes), and the "bottle tree" between the buildings.

Gemeinnuß vor Eigennuß!
Glaube und wisse:der
angefangene Gemeinschaftsbau ist die Zukunft unsrer Kinder.

The meeting hall at Fernheim Colony (shown here in 1935) was opened to the Bruderhof refugees as a place to gather. Note the portrait of Adolf Hitler at the front, and the old German saying on the banner – Gemeinnutz vor Eigennutz! ("common good before private good") – a favorite Nazi slogan.

came from a distance of forty kilometers with their smallest children. Sometimes the gatherings were held outside. Both groups enjoyed singing: they found songs that both knew or taught each other new ones. Music, it seemed, could bring the feistiest political opponents together.

Barriers remained. The people of Menno Colony were particularly conservative and isolated. They did not teach their children geography, and the only book they read was the Bible. Unlike their better educated brethren in Fernheim, however, they were for the most part firm in their pacifism. In general, the colonists made a world-weary impression – "withdrawn and blunt, with few exceptions," Edith wrote. That was not a cause for consternation, however, but a reason to reach out. To quote Edith again:

> We are trying to bring them the social message of Jesus. In spite of their poverty there is great injustice. We feel sorry for them. They have lived here for ten years without a doctor. Every family has lost several children – some as many as six or more – and often the father or mother is missing. Most of them have taken a resigned attitude to these events, for the faith that brings the assurance of life's ultimate victory over all death does not seem particularly strong among them. Perhaps God has sent us here to bring them the message of the kingdom of God.

Emmy wrote:

> Edith and I were helping in the hospital and grew horrified to think about the potential for trachoma and the other illnesses. We decided on certain hygienic measures, but in spite of taking these, we will not be able to completely escape these dangers. We told ourselves, *"Lieber Hakenwurm als Hakenkreuz"* – "Better hookworm than hooked cross (swastika)!"

On January 30, Fritz Kliewer organized a celebration for the anniversary of Hitler's coming to power. The next night, the Bruderhof hosted a singing evening, led by Adolf Braun. After one of the Mennonite ministers led an old hymn, Emmy offered an additional verse she knew from her youth. Paraphrasing Zechariah 8:23, it went:

Ten men from every nation
Shall grasp the robe of a Jew,
Saying, "Come, let us follow;
We have heard God's with you."

Recalling the irony of the situation, Emmy wrote in her diary: "A whole crowd of Mennonite Nazis were standing outside the window, while the Mennonites in the room were singing lustily along with us. Edith rocked with laughter when we got home and said, 'Just think what we put our hosts through today!'"

Later Hardy reminded the Mennonites of their Anabaptist heritage and of their founder, Menno Simons, and his insistence on nonviolence. Adolf and Fritz also exhorted them to return to their roots and challenged them to consider the practice of community of goods. Some of them, like Nikolai Siemens, editor of the *Menno-Blatt*, took the admonition seriously, and at one point the Bruderhof group sensed that opportunities for deeper exchange might be opening. Others, however, including Fritz Kliewer and Julius Legiehn, persisted in arguing that Hitler was promoting Christian values. They claimed that the Bruderhof was merely proselytizing.

5

CHACO

*What the significance of this time of
waiting will have for our future we do
not yet know. It is a time of waiting.*

MARIANNE ZIMMERMANN

SUSI'S FACE was wet with sweat all the time, and her
blouse stuck to her back. There was no escape from the
merciless heat. Even at night—beautiful as the strange sky
was—it did not cool off. Her feet were swollen, making
walking painful, and the heat seemed to sap all her energy.
The children fussed at night and scratched at bug bites.
Open wounds quickly became inflamed. There was a constant shortage of water. It hardly rained, and the wells the
Mennonites had dug yielded only salty, impotable water.
She worried about snakes; some had been seen. A child,
Michael, had even picked one up and waved it triumphantly
over his head: "Look what I found!" It was a deadly coral
snake, and luckily—thank God—he hadn't been bitten.

One day during her noon *siesta*, she opened a sleepy eye
to see a giant lizard, one and a half meters long, creeping

Susi Gravenhorst, a
classmate of Edith
Boecker's at Tübingen
who came to the
Bruderhof in the early
1930s and married
Jan Fros, a Dutchman.

toward her. It reminded her of the hideous creature little
Ebbo had proudly brought to his mother the previous day,
beaming: ten centimeters long, it looked like a flattened
snake, but with an armored back, feet, defined jaws with
many small teeth, and, on its tail, a pair of pincers – an off-
spring of hell, she thought.

There was beauty, too: delicate blue star flowers and on
a thorny cactus, the shiny blossomed queen of the night.
Thousands of white butterflies, whirling like snowflakes
against the blue sky. A flock of brilliant green parrots
streaking overhead.

She looked at the whitewashed mud-brick houses, the
lack of any timber or stones, the arid landscape, the lack of
sweet water, and wondered. She noted how pale and listless

the Mennonite children were – they often seemed to do little more than sit about on their doorsteps, waving little flies away from their eyes. The older children seemed to work all day. She was expecting her second baby. What kind of life would this be for a newborn?

Close by, the indigenous Enlhet tribe had a camp. They were small and stocky, and both men and women went around naked from the waist up. They lived communally, in straw huts, their traditional way of life having been disrupted when Casado's logging operations destroyed their hunting grounds. The Enlhet seemed fascinated by the newcomers, and the Bruderhof members were equally intrigued. If one of the Enlhet received a gift, he would take it back and share it with the tribe: when the Mennonites hired one to work for them and gave him trousers, he returned the next day without them – and refused to wear them until all the other men in the village had a pair too. The Mennonites had taught the natives their German dialect, and it was strange to hear them using it. There were other local tribes too, including a group of hunters whose tall men impressed the newcomers with their erect walk and long black skirts. At night the rhythmic beat of their drums could be heard across the bush.

The community group tried to settle into their new home as quickly as possible, establishing a daily routine for the sake of the young children, and following such Paraguayan customs as a three-hour siesta at midday, when the heat was at its worst. It was surely much easier to work early in the morning or in the evening.

Families set up their quarters in the classrooms that had been allotted to them at the Mennonite school. Some people had beds, but most of the men slept on the floor. A kitchen was set up outside the main building, partly in the open and partly covered by a corrugated iron roof. One of the brothers went to the Mennonite cooperative every morning for milk and eggs. Meals consisted of stew, cooked in a big black kettle. They were eaten outdoors if the weather was good and otherwise in the community center. One day at noon, as everyone stood in line for their bowl of soup, there was a loud scream. A fat, green snake was hanging on a branch above the cauldron.

One of the most pressing questions was how to get water, and as the community considered potential locations for building up a new community, this became one of the most crucial issues. As it was, the Chaco, which had once been covered by ocean, was now sitting on vast aquifers of saltwater. Out of every ten bores, the locals warned them, only one would be sweet. Every evening a wagon rolled through the village with big barrels of dirty water, and everyone came for his allotment. Now the day's washing commenced, beginning with the youngest. Older children had to reuse the water after a younger sibling's bath, and after they were finished, the water was used a third time to launder the family's clothes. By morning, everything was dry and ready to wear again.

During the day, the children were divided into groups by age: thirteen schoolchildren, seven kindergarten children, and twenty toddlers and babies. Kurt built a large

A makeshift kitchen in the Chaco. Sometimes there was only gruel–but no one starved.

playpen for the youngest ones, because it was too dirty and dangerous to let them crawl on the bare ground. Gretel took on the kindergarten group and Marianne the school. Excursions through the thorny underbrush offered exciting discoveries–fossilized seashells in the sand, remnants of the prehistoric sea, exotic butterflies, and a bounty of birds. There were vultures and parrots, wild pigeons, and even a small woodpecker with a bright red head. The wild animals were shy, but not the snakes, which were found uncomfortably close to the community's shelters, especially in the evening.

The narrow paths trodden by the Indians yielded new surprises too: once the children came across an indigenous woman sitting on the ground in a little clearing, weaving. Holding the threads taut with her big toe, she skillfully wove them into bracelets, necklaces, and belts.

<del>-<--->-</del>

For weeks now they had been on the road, and the wear on the children was obvious. They needed the discipline of a regular schedule. As most of the men were out looking at possibilities for shelter (and land to farm), the mothers were left not only to do what housework there was – if it could be called that – but also to take care of the little ones. It was difficult, what with the relentless oppression of the energy-draining heat, and the rashes and fevers, which seemed to beset a new family every day. They were beginning to understand what the Mennonites called tropical

Cooking over an open fire made hot days even hotter.

Laundering clothes and bedding was a full-time chore, especially during epidemics of contagious disease.

madness. Edith wrote in a letter to Hardy, who was away looking at various properties:

> A notable thing about this heat is that it seems to get in the way of inner experiences. It isn't easy to gather inwardly, even just by yourself. The heat has a stupefying effect. Meanwhile the children run wild. Ebbo doesn't listen at all, and it's not easy to educate him; he has no respect for me. There's a great deal of sickness too—lots of malaria and hookworm and fever. Johannes was miserable for days and just lay there.

At the end of each afternoon, parents took their children, washed and readied them for bed, and even took a short stroll, or told a bedtime story. After the children were asleep, the adults ate their meager dinner. To end the evening, they gathered for prayer and to review the problems and joys that had arisen in the course of the day.

One great joy was the arrival of new babies. The births did not proceed without anxiety. What with the exhaustion and stress of the previous weeks of travel, bumpy roads, a lack of nutritious food, and the difficulty of hygiene, it was hardly an ideal setting in which to give birth.

Luckily there was a small, two-room clinic in Filadelfia run by a nurse, Sister Susie Isaac. Here, early in the morning of January 4, Susi Fros gave birth to a little boy, Jan Peter Melchior. A few days later, on January 8, Emily was born to Cecilia Paul, a tiny little girl, weighing less than three pounds.

6

THE SEARCH FOR A HOME

*For here we have no lasting city, but
we seek the city which is to come.*

HEBREWS 13:14

THE MOST PRESSING TASK for the Bruderhof on arriving in the Chaco was finding a place to build homes for some three hundred people. This work began immediately: the men divided into teams, and *Oberschulze* Julius Legiehn arranged for Mennonite men to accompany them as they looked over various options.

On January 8, Fritz Kleiner, Adolf Braun, and Hardy Arnold set out with Legiehn and David Loewen on a two-day expedition. They looked first at camp land a few miles north of Filadelfia, between Village 10 (Rosenort) and Village 9 (Auhagen). The brothers thought this was too small. From there they went on to look at a camp fifteen kilometers northwest of Rosenort. This looked better, but they did not want to commit until they had examined other possibilities. They went down to Schoenbrunn to the southwest, which also seemed possible, although the soil was very sandy.

When they returned, Fritz and Adolf set out again, along with Hans Meier, this time to the south and west, on another two-day expedition. Many years later Hans recalled:

> Some of us started out with a Lengua (Enlhet) chief to find a place. We deliberately turned not only to the company that owned the land, but also to the so-called Indians from whom the land had been stolen. They were very helpful because they understood our longing for community. After riding for several hours on small horses—instead of saddles, we rode on sheepskins—we arrived at a large tract of land which the chief indicated would be a good place for us to settle. As the formal purchase price for the property, which was comprised of several hundred hectares, he asked for only one dollar. Instead of a signed contract, he requested a handshake, which was of more value to him than a written statement.
>
> Accompanying him to his home after this, we found a tree, the lowest branches of which were covered to keep the rain off. All the members of the tribe sat on the ground in a circle around this tree. Apparently it was here that they handed in the spoils of their hunting expeditions or whatever they earned to the oldest woman, who divided and distributed them according to need.
>
> Their world view was fascinating: they believed that the good God of Light reigned during the day, whereas during the night an evil Dark Demon governed. That was why we had heard them beating their drums and singing at night: in order to chase away the darkness.

On January 12, Legiehn took four brothers on a longer trip, toward Hoffnungsfeld. There they split; two brothers

Hans Meier and his wife Margrit (a sister of Trautel Dreher's), at an airfield near Primavera.

looked at other camps to the northeast and at the villages of Menno Colony. Hardy and Fritz went with Legiehn to East Paraguay where, from what they had heard, land was more fertile.

At first they had to backtrack on the route they had traveled at Christmas: all the way back to Km 145, then a train to Puerto Casado, and then a boat back down the river. In Puerto Casado they received a telegram from England announcing the departure of six young men from the Cotswold Bruderhof, their original point of departure. This was a great encouragement – every hand would be put to use immediately for construction.

They arrived in Rosario, a port about a hundred kilometers north of Asunción, in the evening of January 18. From there they went to Friesland, the Mennonite colony that had split from Fernheim. Hardy was immediately struck

Primavera's greenery was a sight for sore eyes after the dreary landscape of the desert-like Chaco.

by the lush greens of East Paraguay, as compared to the arid Chaco. He wrote:

> There is a wealth of natural beauty here—regal palms, woods and meadows and valleys, and the roses—roses! God is leading us. We feel that plainly. It is a matter of building up the church as an embassy of God's kingdom. Tell everyone that, and encourage them if they should flag or weaken. A wonderful task lies before us. May God grant us the strength and courage to hold on so that it succeeds. His kingdom is our goal—nothing less!

Bordering Friesland was an *estancia* belonging to a German, Herr Rutenberg. It seemed that here they had found the Promised Land. Hardy wrote enthusiastically about it:

> How shall I begin to tell you of the wealth of experiences

we have encountered or give you a picture of this area? It is very different from the Chaco. Everything grows more luxuriantly here, the scenery is more beautiful, and it is not as hot. There is water – tons of it! In Friesland there are gardens that were planted two or three years ago on what had been virgin forest, with luxuriously growing fruit trees, banana plantations, mandioca, and cotton – meters high. There are also roses that bloom the whole year, grapes, coffee, sugarcane, melons, and even tobacco. Everything grows much faster than in the Chaco, though the cotton does not yield as well.

The land is hilly, even if the hills are not as high as our home in Germany. The higher terrain is covered with thick forest, whereas the "camp" and fields lie in the lower parts of the land.

On the first day we went through all the villages with the *Oberschulze* of Friesland, Kornelius Kroeker. We were amazed at what had been accomplished in three years in the way of forest-clearing, plowing, building, road-making, their schools, and so on. Everything looks better and is in better order than in Fernheim. Perhaps the main reason is that better timber is available for building. At the same time their income is not as good as Fernheim's because their cotton does not have such a good yield. So they are slowly changing over to other sources of income: corn, and above all, cattle and dairy products.

The next day Herr Görzen, *Schulze* of Landes Krone, took us to a place called Primavera to look over Herr Rutenberg's 7780 hectare property (about 20,000 acres). This is situated on a hill, Loma Hoby, where there is a clearing. Our first impression was: here is our future Bruderhof! This feeling was equally strong in both of us.

The land adjoins Friesland Colony to the west; the main road runs along the north side to the river port of Rosario, which is about fifty-three kilometers away. To the east lies a neighboring estate which at one time also belonged to Herr Rutenberg; and along the southern boundary runs the Tapiracuay River, which drains the whole property. Primavera makes up a rough square almost nine by nine kilometers in size. For two whole days we crisscrossed it on horseback, looking it over until we were exhausted. Aside from being saddle sore, Fritz developed an infection in his foot, and I hurt my arm. But that did not dampen our conviction, which grew from hour to hour, that this is the place for us.

Hardy then went on to summarize the advantages of Primavera over other properties they had considered. He concluded:

> One thing is certain: God is leading us with his strong hand, and whatever happens, we will follow him without interposing our own wishes or deeds. We pray for you all every day, for our six brothers on the high seas, and for our brothers and sisters in England. How we look forward to their coming! The time is urgent. Let us press forward. May God give us courage and strength for building up.

Fritz wrote similarly:

> What we have seen and experienced in the Chaco bears no comparison with the scenic beauty of this area. Here are luxuriant virgin forests, the giant trees twined round with woody lianas, and whole groves of bitter oranges, the fruit

just now ripening, without anybody attending to it. Only
the leaves are used here and there to prepare an extract that
commands a good price for use in soaps and perfumes. Sweet
orange trees are equally prolific, if not more so. The main
harvest time starts in June or July. They simply grow wild,
being propagated by monkeys and parrots.

And the springs! When a young Mennonite from the
Chaco first came to the area where Friesland is now and discovered a spring, they say he drank and drank and sang and
sang, so full of enthusiasm was he. The scenery here fills
mind and heart with joy: the higher parts wooded, the lower
ones grassy, with no bushes or trees – just here and there a
few palm trees of magnificent height.

Hans Meier traveled to Asunción to meet Fritz and Hardy.
There were details to be worked out regarding the purchase,
including the question of whether the privileges promised
them by the government were contingent on their settling
in the Chaco or held also for East Paraguay. Meanwhile
they looked at several other properties before making their
final decision. On January 28, Hardy wrote to the brothers
and sisters in Fernheim:

> Are you agreed that Hans, Fritz, and I, if we feel inner cer-
> tainty that this is the place, act right away? Please send us a
> telegram whether you are in agreement with Primavera.
>
> Have courage; it is for God's kingdom and the building up
> of the church. It is worth waiting for.

Replying a few days later, Edith wrote:

My beloved Hardy...This morning your letter arrived. It's inspiring to hear about springs and roses, hills and a river, how near the capitol city is, and so on. If we are close to Asunción, there are many things we can do to market goods–turnery, fruit juices, jam, and more. Let's hope we will get the necessary permissions, otherwise all the beauty in the world won't help us. But how happy I am that there is natural beauty there, for our children's sake, too. We are made up not only of body and spirit but also of soul, and beauty in nature makes life easier. The absence of malaria in the area is very important, too, and above all the lack of mosquitoes.

This place is a real malarial hotbed. Unfortunately we have not been spared–Susi is no longer the only one. I have it too, as well as all our children. So far, everyone Cyril has tested seems to have it. In fact, we can assume that ninety percent of us have it. It is an insidious disease; it saps your vitality, and in the long run this disease could have a devastating effect. I don't think we should allow the new arrivals to come here.

On the other hand, we talked it over in our meeting last night, and John Hinde said that a thing like malaria cannot possibly prevent God's purpose from being fulfilled–his cause is too great. That was excellent.

The brothers who went to the camp land in Hoffnungs-feld returned today. They are enthusiastic. I am, of course, most enthused about East Paraguay. This place is too desolate for me.

Two Mennonite couples visited us recently. They were moved, most of all by the love they sensed among us. However, they were concerned about our dancing and smoking. As you know, Mennonites are brought up to regard these things as sin. They told us about what they had gone through in Russia and how they had been imprisoned because of their refusal to do military service. On Sunday afternoon I was invited to Sister Susie; she, too, told me about Russia.

The Mennonites here are not clear about military service; many believe a Christian can also be a soldier. Still, there is a movement of heart among them, and a sense of community. This was noticeable on the singing evening we had, where there was considerable participation—more than at the celebration they held for the anniversary of Hitler's ascension to power on January 30…

From time to time we remind one another to be patient. Impatience among adults, as well as the illness, etc., has a negative effect on the children, too, and it has been hard to manage them. Last night Hans-Hermann held a very moving prayer meeting in which we talked about all this and made a new start. As we have experienced so abundantly, God loves us, even though we go through hard times. Joy will overcome! People here are so joyless.

Hans-Hermann Arnold, too, wrote to his brother Hardy on February 3:

Our work situation has been made very difficult by the fact that eight brothers have been at the camp at Rosendorf and then at Hoffnungsfeld, that Alan was away until today, that three sisters had babies and dropped out of the work, and twenty-six of our group have malaria. You can imagine how much this affects the inner life of the community as well, since one becomes extremely tired and lethargic and needs every bit of willpower to get through the day. Everyone is strained to the utmost. But in spite of that, with God's help we have been kept together, and everybody faithfully gives their very best, often on days of up to 110° F.

We all feel these hardships to be attacks, attempting, as they do, to paralyze the work and mission. So we met yesterday to intercede for our brothers in England and for our building up here. We must not slacken, for the whole church community and its reestablishment as a witness is at stake. We feel the urgency at this world hour to gather strength through quiet encounters with Christ, in order to stand completely under his rulership.

That night the members met to consider Hardy's request for input as to the purchase of Primavera. Hans-Hermann wrote again:

We have unanimously agreed to send you the following telegram: "Report received. Stand behind you in unity, love, and expectation. Many have mild malaria; but joy, brotherhood." This message means you should feel completely free to act as you see fit. We are open to accept any place God has destined for our mission and community life, and we trust completely in his leading. We are fully united – united in joy and expectation that you should purchase Primavera, or else a different place, should God lead you so.

Now in Asunción, the three brothers had much to do. Fritz's left foot became swollen and extremely painful, and he had to stay in bed. Hardy and Hans returned to Friesland and Primavera, leaving Fritz in the city. He wrote to his wife on February 8:

Fritz Kleiner with his wife, Sekunda, an artist, a few years before the Bruderhof's expulsion from Nazi Germany.

I've now been in Asunción for a week and a half. I either lie in bed or in a hammock or sit on a chair with my leg raised, trying hard to get it to heal. Day after day I keep hoping for a substantial improvement, but so far it has not come. You will be interested to hear how I contracted it.

When Hardy and I were riding through Rutenberg's lands, we were caught in a downpour. Our feet got wet, and the following day my foot started itching between the toes, and my leg swelled. In the meantime I have consulted three doctors, and each prescribed something different. It is a case of a climate-induced ailment called *sebui*, easily contracted in the rain. It's caused by a little worm that tunnels under your skin, between your toes and under the sole of your foot.

After looking at several other properties near Friesland, Hans and Hardy finally made their decision, and on

February 12 sent a telegram to Fernheim: "Primavera bought. Arrive Saturday at Km 145."

-<--+>-

Meanwhile, the six men who had left England on January 12 were due to arrive in Paraguay. Fritz was at the dock to meet them as the riverboat steamed into Asunción – a joyful reunion. After going through customs, they went to the nearby Hotel Colon, where Fritz told them that they would not be going to the Chaco, but to the new property in East Paraguay. Nineteen-year-old Wolfgang Loewenthal recorded his impressions in his diary:

> After lunch we had a short rest, and Fritz took leave of us to return to his apartment so that he could rest his foot, which was once again very swollen. Nothing became of our attempts to sleep, despite or because of the heat. So we decided to take a tour of the city. There are donkeys, mules, and vendors on all the street corners, women who are remarkable at balancing their wares on their heads, numerous stray dogs running around, dirt, garbage, and excrement on all the side streets…
>
> We observed the local custom of maté drinking. Maté is enjoyed at every hour of the day and night. Mostly four or five people sit around a large wooden, clay, or hard plastic cup and suck the liquid through a brass pipe. When the first one is finished a spoonful of sugar is added, warm water poured on top, and the result passed on to the next one. The cup continues to be passed around the circle in this manner until the

brew has lost all color and flavor. At any rate, a custom that is closely related to the old peace pipe. While waiting for their turn, the others chew their brown cigars. Who knows how long it will take until we are hooked on this brew?

Last night I slept under a mosquito net for the first time. I felt like an elfin prince from a fairy tale under a veil of moonlight. It was so warm, I couldn't sleep for a long time. The sound of trams and cars was an unfamiliar serenade. But finally I fell into a deep sleep.

Hans Meier went back to Asunción, where he bought furniture and machinery. Then he took the train to Buenos Aires, where he planned to meet the second large group that was on its way from England. Hardy, meanwhile, returned to the Chaco. He spent his time on the riverboat drawing up plans for the building up of the new community. Unfortunately, the telegram he had sent announcing his arrival never reached its destination, and he spent three days waiting (rather impatiently) at Km 145. Finally a wagon arrived with Hans-Hermann and Edith. The trio rolled

Paraguayans relaxing in the bush near Primavera.

into Fernheim on February 19. That evening they had a meeting, and Hardy reported on his trip to all the brothers and sisters.

There was plenty to tell Hardy, too, of all that had happened in Filadelfia during his absence. Adults and children alike were recovering from malaria. Adolf was in the hospital with broken ribs – he had tried to stop a runaway team of horses and been injured. Susi was finally feeling stronger again, though her newborn baby was covered with abscesses.

On Sunday, February 24, Hardy held a special service to give thanks for the newest babies. Felix Dreher (who had been born in England, but had not yet received a church blessing), Jan Peter Fros, Emily Paul, Hanske Fros, und Joy Barbara Johnson were brought to the service and laid on a table in the middle of the circle. In this way the parents presented their precious little ones to the community and entrusted them into their care. After that Hardy said a prayer and handed each baby back to his or her parents, commissioning them to bring up their child in the fear of God. It was a great reassurance to the mothers to know that no matter what might lie ahead, their little ones were now in the church's arms.

Over the next week the Bruderhof group held a meeting with the Mennonites almost every night. Hardy spoke about love and unity and about the need for conversion and repentance. One such meeting, held outside, was attended by a thousand people. At another occasion he spoke about the dangers of nationalism and his concern that the Menno-

This Mennonite schoolhouse in Friesland, Village 2, provided a temporary home for Bruderhof women and children while the men erected the first shelters at Primavera.

nite tradition of peace – really, Christ's teaching – was being abandoned. This meeting became quite heated, as Fritz Kliewer and Julius Legiehn defended their position.

Individual Mennonites also came in these days for informal conversation. One elderly couple, along with their widowed daughter, asked if they could go with the Bruderhof group to East Paraguay.

Emmy and Hans-Hermann set out for Friesland, where they planned to meet Fritz and the six new arrivals from England and make arrangements for the group to stay with the Mennonites there until accommodations could be built in Primavera.

On February 25, a farewell evening was held in the center in Filadelfia. *Oberschulze* Legiehn opened the evening:

Llewelyn Harries (left) and Hardy Arnold (center), the eldest son of Eberhard and Emmy Arnold, shortly before the community left England for South America.

Dear friends, it is known to us all in both colonies, Fernheim and Menno, that our friends the Hutterites are leaving us and the Chaco. Many have come to me to ask: "What happened?" So we decided to arrange an evening in which we would give our friends the opportunity to answer all questions. Hardy Arnold is ready to report on what he found in East Paraguay, and he will tell us why they are leaving.

Then Hardy came forward:

When we arrived in Filadelfia on January 2, we did not know where we would find a home for our brotherhood. We decided, before we began building, to examine all the possibilities as thoroughly as possible, both here and in East Paraguay. While we were still looking at camps in the Chaco, Fritz Kleiner and I were sent to East Paraguay. Friesland made a very good impression on us. We were amazed at how well everything grows and how clean and orderly the colony is after only three years. We finally decided on Primavera, a property owned by Herr Rutenberg.

Unless you understand our community, it may not be so easy to understand why we have decided to leave the Chaco. The main reason is a spiritual one. We understand that the Mennonite colonies settled here primarily in order to withdraw from the world. We, however, are driven by the opposite viewpoint. We want to be close to other people because we have a message to bring them. The first Christians lived in cities, in Jerusalem, Corinth, and Rome, in the midst of the people, held together by the Holy Spirit. We cannot hide behind a wall – or a desert – and say, "We don't want the world to touch us!" The world is within us. And there is the danger that a group withdraws into itself and is concerned only for its own blessedness and its own economy. Our task as Christians is a missionary one, to work as yeast among people. This is the main reason why we decided for East Paraguay. Primavera is five days' travel closer to the center of population, to the people whom we love and to whom we want to bring Jesus.

The second reason is also a spiritual one. We consider it unhealthy for the spiritual and cultural life of our community (and economically unsound as well) if we would have only a single means of making a living, such as growing cotton. We would need to plant 300 hectares in order to support a community of 300. We would never manage this, as it would be against our conscience to hire Indians for this work as a cheap labor force. We would rather take them into our community or found a second community with them!

Another economic reason is: you raise cattle and vegetables to supply the military. We have never done this, and I hope we never do. Of course, if a poor hungry soldier comes to us, we will feed him, but to supply the military contradicts our conscience. It has even been said that if the Mennonites hadn't been here, Paraguay would have lost the Chaco War. The government only wants you here for military and political reasons.

There are other reasons which are not unimportant: The climate in East Paraguay is healthier than here. There are very few mosquitoes and practically no malaria. Oranges grow wild, more than one can eat.

I know what you here in Fernheim and your friends in Menno Colony have suffered. It has shaken us deeply, and I have asked myself again and again why this had to be so. I believe God wants to purify you and lead you to repentance, so that you follow Christ more fully. Yet I also believe a great injustice has been done to you. I have heard the same story from many sides, and I believe that if the world knew what happened here, people would be shocked. If better care had been taken, not so many would have died. We will do what we can for you through the Mennonite Central Committee, whose leaders we know. I am not saying this to make you bitter; I believe that what you experienced in Russia and here was also a test or a chastisement, and nothing would make us happier than if our brief sojourn in the Chaco served to shake up your hearts a little. When I saw all the people gathered here I thought, how wonderful it would be if the Holy Spirit would break in here! It would be worth all the need and pain, if we could receive this gift as the first Christians received it in Jerusalem.

One more thing I would like to say: Our hearts are open to you. If you would like to become our brothers and sisters, come to us. We want to thank you for all you have done for us during the past two months, especially your *Oberschulze*. To show our thanks, we are leaving our doctor, Dr. Davies, here until May, and in the future we will try to always have one of our doctors in the Chaco, although I cannot make any promises. If you would wish it, we are ready to have one of our ministers visit each of your villages, and we hope to welcome your young people into our schools. We hope we can often prove our love to you by sending brothers and sisters to visit you. Once more, many thanks and *auf Wiedersehen!*[8]

The decision of the Bruderhof to leave the Chaco was a great disappointment to many of the Fernheim Mennonites, and not only for practical reasons. Nicolai Siemens wrote to the MCC on April 4:

As you have heard, the Hutterites have left our colony for East Paraguay. Some of us who really came to love these tested fellow believers found this very sad. Others, to whom these people spoke too directly into their consciences, were happy when they left. Our little flock that would like to hold faithfully to the teaching of Jesus feels more and more alone. What has happened to our faith!? Lord, have mercy on us in Fernheim! Help us return to the old faith! We will continue to pray. Think of us, dear brothers. We do not want to drown. Pray for us. The prayer of the righteous achieves much if it is earnest.[9]

7

REGROUPING

Build up the city, you builders all,
Joyfully, eagerly, faint not, nor fall;
Concord and love shall in it abide,
Jesus the Lord will be by your side.

FRITZ KLEINER

THE GROUP left behind in England thought constantly of the brothers and sisters who had gone. What might they be experiencing? Phyllis Rabbitts wrote:

> Christmas came and went, but although a mad war in the name of Christ was being waged all round us, we celebrated the anniversary of Christ's birth with increased joy, for had he not been born again in our hearts? Were we not sure that his reign of peace and justice would come, and that although God's judgment was over the whole earth, his love and forgiveness was much greater?
>
> With what tremendous joy we received a cable from our brothers and sisters of their safe arrival in South America. We could do no other than rise and sing, "Now thank we all our God." We eagerly waited for more detailed news of their

Like several other Blue Star vessels that ferried Bruderhof refugees, the Avila Star was later sunk by German torpedoes (in this case, off the Azores, with a loss of 73 lives).

journey. We knew that they had a long journey through the "bush" after the river journey, by train and by wagon. How would they stand it? There were several tiny babies, also six expectant mothers. What might happen to them on such a journey?

While we were awaiting news we read a long letter and medical reports from a doctor who had lived in the interior of Paraguay. What he had to say shook us. He wrote of serious illnesses, of the climate with its unbearable winds, and of many things unheard of to us in England. Also he wrote of the coming of the Mennonites, who on arrival died in hundreds from epidemics, especially that of typhoid. They had arrived in midsummer too. Our hearts were very heavy, almost to breaking. Had we sent our first group to their deaths?

The next day after hearing all this was a Sunday, and we were all gathered for worship. We drew near to each other in faith and hope that God would give us the strength needed in such a sorrowful hour, and that he would care for our loved ones far off in Paraguay. Just before the closing of this hour a cable was brought in containing the wonderful news of their safe arrival in the Chaco and that all health was good. Also that two babies had been born to them, a little son to Susi and Jan and a little daughter to Cecilia and Tom. Our hearts overflowed with joy and thankfulness, and we felt so strongly God's leading in all this.

On February 7, a third group—the largest—left England on the *Avila Star* to join those already in Paraguay. They totaled 158, with a large proportion of little children. Despite the knowledge that two contingents had made it to South America without a single loss, this parting was just as heart wrenching as the previous ones. A diary entry from Liesel Arnold reflects the sentiments shared by many in her situation—that of a young mother with a baby:

> Lately the question came to me repeatedly whether it is right to leave England, where we certainly still have a task. On the other hand, the opening in South America is a true sign from God. Perhaps we are not yet strong and worthy enough to take suffering upon ourselves for Christ.
>
> Will we see one another again here on earth? What will happen to those left in England, and to us, and to those who have traveled out before us? What will happen to anyone in this terrible war where children and mothers are being murdered daily, and whole cities are being leveled?

Behind the tears, however, stood a strong conviction that

there was work do in the strange new land across the Atlantic, and that it was not a time for hesitating or shrinking back. Philip Britts, a young English member, expressed this view in a postcard written the night before the departure.

> On this, the eve of the departure of 158 of our people for Paraguay, leaving behind a group of about 70 souls in England, our hearts are full to choking. For we are more dear to each other than son to mother or daughter to father.
>
> There is one gift of love we can give to each other before we part. That is that we, all of us, those who are going and those who are staying, pledge ourselves anew to the one way, the one fight, the one life, that those who go may know that those behind have taken up the common task anew. And those who stay may know that those who go are bearing the common message. So let us pledge ourselves anew to God and to each other.

The captain and crew were horrified at the large number of little children brought onto the ocean liner. How could they hope to save them in case of disaster? It was a question best not thought about. As always, humor helped. Brian Trapnell, who traveled with his wife and young son, wrote letters home to his parents and made light of the crossing – at least of being seasick:

> Day after day we pitched and rolled heavily, and seasickness took its unfailing toll. After one day almost completely *hors de combat* one gradually began to realize once more that life, after all, had something to offer. For a day or two afterwards one experienced qualms about proceeding into breakfast.

Presumably, after lying in bed all night, one has to find one's sealegs afresh each morning. For over a week, we rolled very heavily all day and all night. At meals, trays were frequently thrown onto the floor with resounding crashes, and quite a lot of crockery must have been broken. During the night one had considerable difficulty in remaining fixed in bed, and was one careless enough to leave anything loose on the racks or hand basins, it would be surely pitched onto the floor during the course of the night, there to roll backwards and forwards with each roll of the ship. Once one had got over the affects of *mal de mer* and could laugh at the efforts of the ship to throw one, it was not without a certain amount of humor, but after several days it did become somewhat of a nuisance, and one longed for more stable footing.

The most memorable event of that voyage was the birth of a baby to Winifred Dyroff. In the mother's own words:

After nine days of stormy weather, I was taken to what was known as "the Duchess Suite," an elegant two-roomed apartment, and there, on February 17, at 4 o'clock in the afternoon, my little daughter, my first child, was born. The weather changed dramatically about two hours before her birth, giving place to blue skies and warm sunshine. As we later heard from the captain, we were near to Tenerife, one of the Canary Islands, when the baby was born. The sailors all said the birth of a baby on board was a good omen and that this voyage would now be a safe one. The first to congratulate my husband, August, was the captain, who asked what we intended to name the baby and said we should not forget that because she was born on a British ship she was

Winifred Dyroff with her daughter Avila, who was born on the transatlantic crossing and named after the ship.

a British citizen. August suggested Avila and the captain added my name. So she became Avila Winifred. I received several gifts from captain and crew – a silver spoon, a hand-hammered pewter beer mug, a plastic teaset, and a beautiful mohair blanket. For many days different members of the crew knocked on the door of the suite, asking to see the baby. The ship's doctor was very proud: "First baby I've delivered in fifteen years and the very first ever on this ship!"

Julia, a sister from Switzerland who acted as Winifred's

nurse, stood guard in the cabin doorway. When she told the captain that the mother could not have visitors yet, he answered, "I am in charge of this ship!" and marched in.

When the ship reached Buenos Aires, Hans Meier was there again to meet them. He welcomed the group to South America and told them that they would not be going to the Chaco but to Primavera. Like the previous groups, they left the *Avila Star* in Buenos Aires and boarded a crowded steamboat for the next leg of the journey. Hans traveled with them. Brian was kept busy washing the diapers and hanging them on lines stretched across the deck, while his wife, Nancy, prepared bottles for her son and the other babies from powdered milk and boiled water. (The group's mothers had been encouraged by an English doctor who had been in the tropics to stop nursing their babies as they would need all their energy to survive. But now their babies were dependent on formula, which was difficult to obtain.) Several times after Nancy had waited for the water to boil for ten minutes, in order to kill any germs, she saw to her consternation that the Paraguayans were using it to make their maté!

Brian reported on the arrival in Asunción:

We did not see much of Asunción, but what we did see gave us a poor impression. The police themselves we found to be a very slipshod lot of men, down-at-the-heel and shabby. After a long wait we were all "dossiered" and "fingerprinted," and marked down as potential criminals.

At Asunción we were transferred to a barge for the remainder of the journey to Puerto Rosario. Soon we were taken in

Brian Trapnell, an English Quaker
who joined the Bruderhof in 1937,
with his son Peter.

tow by a little tugboat to a large cargo vessel the *Aguaray*,
which was to tow us on up the river. Darkness fell, and at
the same time a storm broke, and torrential rain ensued. The
men had barely finished making the barge fast to the side of
the *Aguaray* when this happened, and they quickly tried to rig
up a second sheet over an uncovered part of the deck where
a lot of our hand luggage was stacked. We quickly opened
the empty hold and bundled the women and children down
a ladder, throwing the dry and not so wet mattresses in after
them. Meanwhile everyone did the best they could to salvage
as much as possible from the rain which blew in under the
sheets and through holes so that all the men were quite wet
or at least decidedly damp.

One of the sisters said about this experience: "We had been
reading marvelous stories by Karl May that had awakened

Walking the gangplank at Puerto Rosario was the easy part. Getting heavy luggage on or off the boat was a different story.

the spirit of adventure in us. You can read Karl May comfortably in bed, but here we had a reality check. We lay on the floor like sardines. In the morning we were all remarkably changed, covered with red spots."

To continue Brian's letter:

The rain, accompanied by tropical thunder and lightning, continued more or less all the night. Sleep was well-nigh impossible. The captain of the barge — a huge Italian — and his men did their best for us. We had been led to believe the journey to Puerto Rosario would only take eight hours, but actually we were about double this time en route. We were hourly expecting to reach our destination and were very disappointed at the slowness of our progress.

Morning came and a slight improvement in the weather. The women and children came up on deck, and we had breakfast as best we could on the dry hatch. Cooking was done on a small galley fire. The day wore on, and, at last, about 2 P.M. we were told we were nearing Puerto Rosario. Soon, we arrived off a flight of brick steps running up the mud bank of the river. This was the "port"! We were very disappointed when we heard we should have to remain on the barge a second night, but we made the best of it. It was still raining occasionally, and everything was damp, but we had a slightly better night. On the following morning, Thursday, March 13, we rose and breakfasted early, and then the men carried all the hand luggage, blankets, etc., ashore and up the brick steps to where the first of the Mennonite carts were awaiting. All the women and children and some of the men were then dispatched, five or six to a wagon usually. I said farewell to Nancy, her mother, and little Peter, as I had to remain until we had unloaded the cargo and got it up the steps on to the mainland.

Hans Meier also took leave of the large group. He continued north to Puerto Casado, planning to join Margrit, Cyril, and the others in Filadelfia and accompany them to Primavera. When his train arrived at Km 145, there was no one to meet him. Impatient, he decided to set out on foot—and made it, though not without the help of an indigenous tribe who befriended him along the way and treated his blisters with an ointment made from lizard tail.

◄-‹--›-►

Timber for building was dragged out of the jungle that surrounded Primavera.

Meanwhile, Fritz and the six brothers who had left England in January worked feverishly to prepare accommodations for everyone headed their way: the group of 80 from the Chaco as well as the group of 159 from England. It might have seemed an impossible task to some, but not to Fritz. A hardworking blacksmith and a zealous taskmaster, he had joined the community in Germany, where he had been recruited for a building project. Later, in England, he had headed up the construction of several stone houses designed in the local Cotswold style. Now they were in a new country with different building materials, and again Fritz was to oversee the work.

They built first a little wooden house, divided equally in half, with a room and a veranda. This was to be the nursery. The completion of the roof was celebrated on February 27. Wolfgang noted in his diary: "Every possible occasion to celebrate is eagerly embraced. Life itself is a celebration."

On March 4, Emmy and Hans-Hermann arrived in Friesland – the first contingent from the Chaco. So busy were
the brothers with the building, that they did not have time
to meet the arrivals. Characteristically, Fritz left a note:

> Dear Emmy and Hans-Hermann!
>
> A heartfelt welcome! We hope that when you have re-
> covered from the exertions of the journey, we will be able
> to welcome you to the new home now coming into being.
> We hope you are well and cheerful. I would so much have
> liked to receive you in Friesland, but the building is the most
> important thing now. I keep thinking of the song, "Arise and
> build up Zion," especially the lines: "They must all have a
> place to live in Zion and quench their thirst with us at the well
> of life." I am hoping that by the middle or at latest the end
> of this week the first well will be ready so that we can have
> water for washing. I am so glad you are coming.
>
> Unity, your brother Fritz

Hans Meier and Fritz had looked over the property and
decided on the location to start building: Isla Margarita,
about two miles from Herr Rutenberg's house in Loma
Hoby (Blue Knoll); he was still living there. Isla Margarita
was on a small hill, a high "camp" or prairie, with three
wooded glades. At the southern end it merged into a forest,
with many tall orange trees.

◅–▻

Friesland, the Mennonite Colony where the arrivals from
the Chaco were to stay until sufficient housing was in place,
was set up similarly to Fernheim and Menno–that is, it
consisted of several villages. The Bruderhof group was
to stay in Village 3 (Central) and Village 2 (Grossweide).
Hans-Hermann and Emmy looked at the classrooms in
the school, where the group was to sleep, and got a list of
Mennonite families who were willing to host them, some
in other villages.

Meanwhile the Chaco group began packing once more.
Joy in the prospect of a new home spurred them on. With
them would travel Johann Warkentin and his wife from the
village of Friedensruh, and their thirty-one-year-old widowed daughter Käthe Penner. *Oberschulze* Legiehn reported to the MCC in a letter written March 22:

> A family from Fernheim, Johann Warkentin with his wife and
> daughter, widow Penner, joined the Hutterites and left Fern-
> heim. The proceeds from the liquidation of their property
> will go to paying off our debt to MCC. We gave this family
> the freedom to leave, since they are old and a widow. There
> were other families in Fernheim who wanted to join the Hut-
> terites; we did not allow them to go until MCC states its po-
> sition on this matter. But today these families have calmed
> down again. The Hutterites really proselytized among our
> people for their community. The actions of the Hutterites
> have certainly given some of the settlers of Fernheim a lot to
> think about.[10]

Two trucks had been hired to drive everyone back to

During their first year in Paraguay, Bruderhof travelers depended heavily on Mennonite wagoners, as shown here. The woman is Connie Barron (later Hundhammer).

Km 145, and there they once again boarded the little train for Puerto Casado. Again they found themselves on a riverboat. At Rosario they were met by Mennonites who drove them along the bumpy wagon road to Friesland. Marianne described the trip:

As we drove further east, the palms grew higher, the meadows more lush. We drove into the woods. Evening had fallen, and in the moonlight we recognized the silhouettes of new trees hung with twisted lianas. We were in the dense, romantic jungle. We spent the night in the open on a little hill. When we looked around in the morning, it actually reminded us of Germany. The children ran excitedly to a little pond where black ducks were swimming. Next to it stood an orange tree with unripe, green oranges – like at home we would have an apple tree. The wagons drove up and down hills, through

woods and camp. I enjoyed the landscape, and the children
were excited about the flowers and oranges that we passed.

The Chaco group set up camp in Friesland. Unfortunately,
it seemed that negative gossip had preceded them, and they
never had the same heart-to-heart encounters here as they
had had in Fernheim. Trautel's impressions convey the
mood:

> The schoolhouse has been put at our disposal, but no laden
> tables await us, no loving hands move to receive us. We must
> pull ourselves together after the tiring journey to make ev-
> erything ready. We spent the first night outside under the
> beautiful starry heavens. The atmosphere in the schoolhouse,
> where a picture of Hitler hangs on the wall, was most oppres-
> sive. O blessed sleep under the open skies!

A week later the group of 159 arrived from England, and
with them an enormous quantity of luggage. The ships of
the Blue Star Line traveled empty to South America, so
there was unlimited space in the hold for freight. In England, the men had packed up all the furniture and whatever else they thought the group might need in a new
country, from farm machinery, a large washing machine,
and a printing press, to library books and the writings of
Eberhard Arnold, the community's founder. All of this had
been loaded from the ship to the riverboat, and now had to
be hauled up the bank and loaded onto wagons to be taken
to Primavera. Brian wrote:

This was a job one could never forget. After five weeks of almost complete idleness, to have to trundle huge packing cases varying from 1 to 12 or 13 cwt. [hundredweight = 100 lbs.] up a flight of steps, with a tropical sun pouring down on one, was certainly no joke. We worked the whole day after seeing the others off. Spent an uncomfortable night on the hard hatches of the barge, and only completed the job in the afternoon of the second day. The cases were unloaded from the hold by the barge's men with a steam winch and dumped on to a stage of planks laid between the barge and the shore. Two, three, four or even more men then took charge and rolled the case up the steps and along the ground on top of the bank and stacked it on a big pile. The more urgent packages such as beds, bedding, personal effects were put on one side and loaded up on Mennonite carts. Meanwhile the captain of the barge continually exhorted us with cries of "Tumbar, tumbar."

Eventually all was unloaded. We decided to spend the night in the nearby village of Puerto Rosario, leaving three of our number to stay with and look after the cases. We stayed at the house of a German settler, where we had a good supper, sang songs, etc. Here we got our first taste of mosquitoes, or, rather, they got their first taste of us! Up with the dawn, we set off early. It was another damp, slightly drizzly morning, and the place looked very miserable. The "roads" were all potholes filled with water, deep ruts, etc. We stopped once or twice at friends' houses, had oranges or bananas, etc. Night fell and, at first, it was very dark until the moon rose. About 9:00 P.M. we stopped by the edge of a forest and after having something to eat, lay down to rest under a big tree. It was a restless night, and we were glad of the dawn so that we could

A Mennonite driver in front of his wagon, with Bruderhof women and children on board. Rough roads caused constant jolting and added to the anxiety of the many pregnant mothers.

continue with the journey in the hope of being soon reunited with our families.

The men arrived in Friesland at noon and found their families in Village 2. They were centered at the school with a temporary kitchen set up in the garden of a house on the opposite side of the road. Some were hosted by families up and down the village, but all came to the school for work, meals, and meetings. Laundry work was in full swing, washing and drying out everything that had got damp in the deluge on the barge.

On the following day most of the men went up to Primavera itself, a journey of some seven or eight miles. Brian described:

Coming out of the last forest on the way up, we got our first glimpse of "Isla Margarita," the site of the new Bruderhof. It was just a hill, or piece of high camp land, with one or two "forest islands" on it, and small clumps of trees. We were given a great welcome by Fritz and the others. Part of a small wood island had already been cleared and a small house built. Nearby was a corrugated-iron-roofed shelter which served as a "dining hall," and a place for meetings, etc. On the fringe of the wood, with a truly lovely view over a far stretch of camp land flanked on either side by forests, stood the so-called "Gallop Hut," so named for the speed with which it had been erected. Here on raised platforms were our sleeping quarters. A well was in process of being sunk, but otherwise all water had to be carted from a spring about a mile away. So we settled down to work in Primavera, rising at dawn – and very beautiful were the dawns – and working hard all day, except for the siesta hours at midday. In the evenings we usually had a short meeting and so got early to bed.

<<-->>

On February 14, another small group set out from England, consisting of Peter and Anni Mathis with their five small children and grandmother, Nona; Phyllis Rabbitts; and Elkan and Gertrud Sondheimer. Herr Sondheimer had been the community's attorney in Germany; now, as a Jew, he was eager to leave Europe. Phyllis wrote:

The journey from the Cotswold was commenced early one evening, the first part by car and the rest by train to Glasgow

Phyllis Rabbitts (later Woolston), an
English nurse whose letters provide
some of the most vivid accounts of
daily life during the Bruderhof's
first months in Paraguay.

docks. We had much to occupy our thoughts as we sped
northwards. The hurried and somewhat complicated departure from England I found somewhat unsettling, and trying
to sleep in the night-express train as it tore along through
country and town and the mountainous north did not help
much. Thoughts crowded in upon me. My whole world
seemed to have turned upside down during the past eighteen
months. When I first decided to visit the Bruderhof, I little
dreamed what an inward and outward change to my life it
would bring. I, who had always been so wedded to my home
and folk and country, was about to leave it all, perhaps forever and this gladly to do for the sake of the cause. One felt
deep within one the power of the Spirit that such could be.

The voyage across the Atlantic was a new experience for
us. So many days on the ocean without sight of land, it made
one realize the vastness of the sea and how dependent we
were on God's mercy to take us over in safety. The same ship,
the *Andalucia*, had taken our first group over. The stewards

and stewardesses spoke often to us about our brothers and sisters and made many inquiries as to their welfare. They had also heard that our second large group had traveled on the *Amida* instead of the *Avila,* and as the *Amida* had gone down with all hands—not one saved—they thought that it was our people who had perished. This they said to me on the first day of our voyage, and it was a terrible shock until the date of sailing was mentioned. A similar shock came on the last day of voyage, when the ship's doctor gave a false rumor that several of our women had died on the river steamer journey. We did not know if this were true until we reached Asunción and met Bruce and Hans Meier.

Nona, Anni and Peter, and their five children, and I drew close as the days went by. Giovanni, our youngest—Peter and Anni's baby of seven months—attracted much attention. I think it was because he was always so happy, one rarely heard him cry. He delighted us with his baby prattle and laughter, which could be heard from quite a distance. This joyful contentment of his lasted all the journey, and one felt it did not spring only from his good health. This was, by the way, quite remarkable because of the difficulties we encountered in getting the right food for him until we reached Asunción. One just felt that Giovanni's joy went deeper than mere good health, and it was not surprising that one passenger who took a special interest in him likened him to the Christchild. I remember having similar thoughts about him, and once a momentary doubt came to me as to whether he would be given us for long, but to see him so healthy helped me to dismiss such a doubt as quickly as it came. Later on, after our arrival in Paraguay, I was to be vividly reminded of this when God called Giovanni back to him...

Most evenings after supper and a little talk with Father and
Mother Sondheimer, Peter, Anni, Nona, and I met together
in one of our rooms for a little quiet fellowship, and this we
appreciated after the strange life of the day. Sometimes we
would sing together or just sit in silence, and sometimes Peter
would read to us.

We had great joy, on reaching Rio, to hear that two days
before, the *Avila Star* had called there, so we knew then that
our large group had also a safe journey and our hearts almost
overflowed with gratitude. We hoped that we might find them
all waiting at Buenos Aires, so we begrudged every hour that
kept us back. But we did not leave Rio till next morning, and
later our ship spent several hours at Montevideo.

Father and Mother Sondheimer, who had accompanied us
from the Cotswold Bruderhof and were en route for New
York, left us at Montevideo, where they were to await a ship
for North America. The last week had been a very depressing one for them; they seemed to suddenly realize that they
were parting from their friends, and they were full of doubts
and worries about their future. One felt they were in the grip
of a hopeless despair. This saddened us. We longed that they
and indeed the whole world should share the joy we felt at
being spared the dangers of our journey that we might work
again in Christ's cause. And so it was they left us in misery
and doubt.

Next morning we found ourselves in Buenos Aires, and
we learned from a letter handed to us that the large group
had already left by steamer to go up the river and that it was
not possible to wait for us. But the rest of the news in the
letter gave us great joy and excitement because it told us
that our first group had found new land for the site for our

Bruderhof and not nearly so far inland as the Chaco. It was to be Primavera, East Paraguay, and the land chosen was wooded and slightly hilly and altogether much healthier. It was a wonderful piece of news and it thrilled us. Of course there would be difficulties in front of us in whatever part of Paraguay we took our abode, but nothing seemed to matter so long as we were reunited and could together commence to rebuild our Bruderhof.

The days we spent on the river steamer really did seem long and almost dreary; now that we were so far on our way, we grew quite impatient in our desire to be united once more with those gone before, so each hour's delay fretted us. The children found various things to interest them, and there was great excitement when they spotted a crocodile – and we saw quite a number of them.

We found Asunción to be a city which spoke of past glories; we knew it was due to the aftermath of war. During our walks through the town, we saw and heard more than plenty to depress us for a long time. What kind of new problems would there be for us in this new country? We had left Europe in the heat of its war, with all the suffering and trouble which war brings, where men's minds were becoming more and more saturated with the war fever and less and less receptive to our message. And now here we were arriving in a new country, amongst a different kind of people laid low by the havoc and devastation of their past war. What had it to say to us? These thoughts filled our minds during those few days of waiting, and we longed more than ever to get on with the task of rebuilding our Bruderhof.

From Asunción we went by boat to Rosario, then a two-day journey by Mennonite wagon to Friesland. Anni and I sat in deck chairs all night; the children slept on the floor. We experienced a tropical storm that soaked us to the skin and covered us with mud, and in such a state did we arrive! The luggage wagon got stuck, so we had nothing to change into when we got to the village, and all the brothers and sisters that were already there had nothing to spare to lend us. But we were together again, and that was wonderful.

8

FIRST LOSSES

The fact that children have to suffer is very strange. It is as if they are bearing someone else's guilt, as if they are suffering because of the fall of creation, as if they are paying the wages of sin—sin in which they have taken no part. I believe that the suffering of children has a close connection with the greatest suffering ever endured, Christ's suffering for lost creation, for they are closest to the heart of Jesus, and he points to them as an example for us. I believe the suffering of an innocent child has great significance.

HEINI ARNOLD

THERE WERE NOW 260 people divided between Primavera and the Friesland villages, including about 130 children, most of them quite young. There was no doctor: assuming that two more, Ruth Land and Margaret Stern, were arriving shortly, Cyril Davies had been asked to remain in the Chaco.

Elfriede Braun (later Barron) with two newborn babies. Aside from contagious diseases spread by flies and mosquitoes, the constant heat and dust—not to mention a lack of enclosed shelters—made childcare a daily challenge.

Village 2 consisted of houses surrounded by vegetable patches, built in a long line along one side of a road. Across the school yard and through a belt of trees lay the Mennonite cemetery. One day one of the Bruderhof mothers who was walking there commented on the large number of children's graves. The woman tending them looked at her intently: "Those are from when we first arrived. It will happen to you too." The Mennonite children in Friesland also had inflamed eyes—in fact, the eyelids of many were so swollen that they had turned inside out and their eyes were filled with pus.

Mothers with newborns were billeted among Mennonite families. The others squeezed into the schoolhouse. It had three large rooms and a wide veranda along the front facing the playground and woods. In two of the rooms the men built a raised platform, where the children slept in a long row. Hans Meier had bought a pile of collapsible beds in Buenos Aires, which the adults used. In the daytime they were stacked away.

The third room was arranged as a baby room. At one corner was the "surgery," where Trautel attended to the children's tropical sores. To cheer them up, she would paint a little flower or a heart or a star on the backs of their hands with iodine.

Because it was extremely crowded, people spent as much time as possible outside. When the weather was good, they made use of trestle tables under the trees in the school yard. As in the Chaco, the cooking was done outside in big cauldrons and kettles on open fires. Meanwhile the children were occupied in the woods where it was shady. The ground was sandy, and they were content to play with sand, water, and sticks. Several of the women were trained as kindergarten teachers. With a wealth of nursery rhymes and simple games at their fingertips, they tried to distract the children and keep them happy in the heat.

In these difficult conditions, people became irritable and impatient with one another and with their disobedient children. The Warkentin family, who had come with the brothers and sisters from Fernheim, became discouraged and returned to the Chaco. John Hinde wrote: "The sisters had to cope with all these little children without their husbands. They were crowded and had to cook and do the washing of clothes and dishes under very primitive conditions out of doors. I must confess to my shame that it was a relief when I went up to Primavera for the real pioneering with the men."

Hardy was almost continually on horseback, trying to keep the three groups—one in Primavera and two in the Mennonite villages—in touch with one another. Money was running out—some of the brothers had spent too freely on the voyage, and a lot of household necessities and equipment had been purchased. Hardy was disappointed that his brother Heini had not arrived with the large group—he had been counting on his help for both spiritual and practical oversight. He had also been hoping that the community's doctors, Ruth and Margaret, would be there by now, but they had not arrived either.

Those who had been in the Chaco brought with them malaria and conjunctivitis, an inflammation of the eyes, and the children who had just arrived from England were soon infected. In addition, many came down with diarrhea. Hygiene and washing facilities were primitive, and care was difficult. Luckily they had Moni Barth, Emmy's sister, who had crossed the Atlantic in the second large group with her husband, Georg, and their three sons. Moni was an experienced nurse and midwife. She had served as a Red Cross nurse on the front during World War I, so she knew what could be done in primitive conditions.

Families with the youngest babies and expectant mothers, along with the nurses—Emmy, Moni, and Phyllis—were stationed in Village 2. Meanwhile, in Village 3, Sophie

Löber and Cecilia Paul—both of them young mothers—
were staying in a cabin with five infants. They all had
conjunctivitis and diarrhea. Sophie was worried about her
Joachim, who had been sick already back in England and
was now weaker and more lethargic than ever.

Late one evening, after the other mothers had settled
their babies and gone back to their children in the school,
Sophie was startled by a quiet moan. She jumped out of bed
and found Irmgard Keiderling's son, Daniel, panting for
breath. His left arm was cold and damp. She alerted Cecilia
and ran to get help. Outside the cabin, a herd of cows had
lain down across the village road, but Sophie forgot her
fears and scrambled over them. She woke Hardy and Edith
and Irmgard. Someone went to notify Karl, his father, in
Primavera, and Moni in Village 2. Sophie recalled:

> A small circle gathered around the little boy who was appar-
> ently dying before our eyes. For many hours we stood in the
> small room, in which there were four other baby beds. The
> door was wide open. It was an oppressive, sultry night. We
> waited from hour to hour. When would Karl come? When
> would Moni come? It was a heartbreaking hour. We were
> helpless. When Moni arrived towards 4:00 in the morning,
> the little boy had borne his suffering to the end. We stood
> bewildered as if we could not grasp it. And yet, inexplicably,
> God had spoken.

It was Sunday, March 30—just two weeks since Karl and
Irmgard and their eight children had arrived with the large
group. They were stunned. They had known that they

Karl and Irmgard Keiderling, members of the community from its first years in
Sannerz, with their children, shown here ca. 1946.

would meet adversities when they undertook such a great
journey, but the reality came unexpectedly.

Daniel's big brother Ulrich, ten years old, was walking with a friend from the other village. They met Moni
on horseback and noticed that she looked at them sadly.
Then Karl came out to meet them. He took Ulrich by the
hand and led him into the house, where his brother lay as
if asleep.

Now the community gathered – the men, who had come
down for the weekend, and the women and older children
from scattered homes and villages. They were quiet; a feeling of anxiety seemed to hang in the air. Balz Trümpi an-
nounced the heavy news. Each mother's heart trembled as
she thought of her own little ones.

In the tropical heat, the little body had to be buried quickly. Fritz helped Karl build a tiny coffin, and the brothers in-
terrupted their building work to decide on the location for
the community's burial ground – and to dig a grave.

The next day Hardy and Edith went with the Keiderling
family and the little coffin up to Primavera. All the brothers joined them at the graveside at the forest edge, a short
distance from the building site.

⊰⊷⊱

The following day, April 1, Nellie Stevenson gave birth
to her first child, a little girl whom she named Primavera
Faith. Nellie, a Dutch woman, had married Alan the previous June. The months in the Chaco had been especially
difficult for her. Her sensitive skin blistered in the tropical
heat, and she had struggled with fear and discouragement.
Now in Friesland it sometimes seemed even harder.

Alan had worked as a salesman for various companies
in England before joining the Cotswold Bruderhof, and he
served the community for years by overseeing its finances.
He wrote Nellie notes from Primavera:

> As you are well aware, your husband is very impractical, and
> I have felt this way deeply in the last two weeks. It is not easy
> for me, as I have had almost no practical training at all, and
> like you I want to do my best. For some days I was depressed
> because I could not help more.
>
> One thing that I am very glad about is our closeness to

Alan Stevenson, an Englishman,
with his Dutch wife, Nellie, and
their daughter, Primavera.

nature. Have you seen the skies at nighttime? And the lightning?

Just a few words of comfort, which I hope you will receive
safely. Yesterday I was very sad to leave you, but on the other
hand I always think of it as an honor to take part in the actual
building up of our new home. I only wish that you were here
too to experience these first days. I am sending this letter in
a few minutes with a man from your village but will write
again shortly.

    Darling, it is not easy for any of us at the moment — fam-
ily life is upset — the sun is hot — there is hardly room to
move — and so on. Nevertheless I feel very strongly bound to
you at the moment, and I know that when our baby comes,

we shall be even more strongly united. Family life really begins when the first child comes! The name (very important) will be given to us I am sure—but we must of course look for it. Many names would be suitable, and I think a suitable name would be connected with our new home or whatever we are experiencing at the moment. Just now we are all experiencing joy—firstly because of the reuniting with everybody from England and then because of our new home, and in a certain sense, new life.

We are all working hard so that in a few weeks everybody can come here. Don't forget to send for me as soon as anything happens, as I want to be there when our first daughter (or son) is born.

With very much love, my sweetheart, your Alan

The time finally came. Phyllis helped Nellie to one of the Mennonite homes and sent a message for Alan to come down. There were complications, and Phyllis tried to remember what she had learned in her midwifery training—this was a situation she had not dealt with before, and there was no doctor. When the little girl was born, she appeared lifeless. But finally she gave a cry and started to breathe. Nellie's mother, who attended the birth, expressed her emotions in a card she penned to her daughter:

> Great, quiet joy. Radiant expectation,
> Interrupted only once by doubting fear.
> Then: hours of pain lashing the body…
> Pain unbearable; fear unbearable:
> God, God—God! Give thy help!

God heard and gave us our little girl, Primavera.
We praise and thank him for his love.
We name her also Faith – trust in God.

Lord, may we never forget this hour of joy and grief,
Never become unfaithful.

The following Sunday was Palm Sunday, the beginning
of Holy Week. Once more the community gathered and
prayed for spiritual strength to bear whatever might lie
ahead.

There was still much sickness. Mosquitoes and tiny flies
continued to plague adults and children alike, and if the
bites were scratched open, they tended to get infected.
Even worse was an insect that crawled under the skin to
lay its eggs. In addition, almost all the children and even
some adults were suffering from conjunctivitis and needed
to have their eyes treated twice a day with painful drops,
a job that kept two women busy all day. On top of all this,
there was epidemic diarrhea. Several of the babies seemed
almost as sick as Daniel had been.

Giovanni Mathis, for instance, was wasting away. He
had been born two days after Daniel. Their mothers had
been together in the maternity house at the Cotswold Bruderhof back in England and had dreamed of their sons
growing up together. Now Daniel was dead, and Giovanni
so thin you could see his bones. His six-year-old brother
Pete spent hours by his side trying to keep the flies off his
face. Giovanni's big, brown eyes looked pleadingly at his
mother as if to say, "Can't you help me?" Sisters and chil-

Peter and Anni Mathis and their children on the transatlantic crossing. Giovanni (in Anni's arms) was one of the first babies to succumb to the ravages of poor nutrition and disease in Paraguay.

dren gathered outside the hut to sing songs of encouragement and faith. Anni cradled her child on her lap, coaxing him, calling him, singing to him. Moni was at her side, but there was nothing she could do.

In Primavera the baby's father, Peter, heard that he was sick. Unable to find a horse, he walked the seven miles and went directly to the hut where the sick child lay. With eyes for no one else, he strode into the baby's room and knelt at Anni's side. "Giovanni! Giovanni!" he called in anguish. The baby's breaths grew shallower and slower. "Giovanni!" But he was gone.

Hardy and Edith prepared their own small space for the wake. A kerosene lamp hung on the wall next to the baby's bed, and Sophie picked three roses from a garden outside one of the Mennonite houses to decorate the room.

The next morning the brothers came down from Primavera to bring up their families from Village 3. It should have been a day of rejoicing—the women and children were finally to see their new home—but they drove in silence. Emmy stayed back with Peter and Anni until Fritz brought the coffin.

As they waited, one of the Mennonite women stopped by. She had shown sympathy to the ailing child, but the only comfort she could offer Anni was bleak: "We lost our husbands. Be glad you lost only a child." Anni stared at her through her tears. Suffering has hardened her heart, she thought.

In the late afternoon they took the long wagon trip up to Primavera. By the time of the actual burial, night had fallen. The moon shone as the community gathered around the second little grave. Karl helped Peter lower the coffin, and silently, in twos and threes, the brothers took turns filling the grave. Peter concluded the simple service by speaking to the community of the coming kingdom when all tears would be dried and of his certainty in the resurrection.

-<-+->-

Emmy Arnold (right) with her sister Monika "Moni" Barth. A nurse who tended to soldiers during World War I (and was decorated for her bravery on the front lines), Moni was also a skilled midwife.

After the burial, Moni and Emmy came down again to Friesland. "I'm not going to bury another child," Moni said determinedly. She examined each child and encouraged the mothers to keep offering their children enough fluids. She insisted that Brian Trapnell come down from Primavera to support Nancy, as their little boy, Peter, was also close to death. She herself stayed up all night, forcing the children to swallow sugar water or broth every half hour. Emmy told the sisters: "We have to face this together. Perhaps things will get even worse. Let us stand together and trust that God has his hand over us."

Meanwhile a telegram was sent to Cyril in the Chaco, advising him that his medical services were urgently needed in Friesland: "A second child has died. Come immediately."

The next day was Good Friday, which the community observed as a day of silence, remembering Jesus' suffering. The group in Primavera and the group in Village 2 did only necessary work and spent the rest of the day in quiet contemplation, pondering the mystery of death and suffering. It was all the more powerful, on Easter morning, to gather and sing the triumphant old carols proclaiming Christ's resurrection.

9

PRIMAVERA

No citadel
no glimmering Jerusalem
no golden city

but it is first seen from afar.

And a long journey
and a steep way
and a treacherous, pain-weary,
siren-taunted voyage
lie between.

JANE TYSON CLEMENT

THE MEN were working as hard and as fast as they could to build shelters at Isla Margarita. They could not continue in Friesland much longer, as the Mennonite school year was about to begin, and they needed their classrooms back. Fritz's wife, Sekunda, was one of the first to move out of the schoolhouse. Bringing her six children along, she set up house in the first hut that was ready – and began caring

Buildings under construction at Primavera. Even when finished, they provided spartan quarters: large halls divided into family rooms by means of sheets and blankets.

for the sixty men stationed there as well, especially those who were suffering from malaria and tropical sores.

Rudi and Wolfgang dug a well: one lowered the other on a rope, to fill bucket after bucket with dirt; the other remained at ground level to haul up the filled buckets. It was hard, dangerous work: once the whole pulley contraption came crashing down, and Wolfgang was almost killed.

Other men were busy felling trees, hauling the logs out of the forest with oxen, and then cutting them into posts. Rafters were made from the long, straight *mbavú* trees and were carried out on the shoulders of three men. Laths were made of bamboo, which was felled and fetched from several miles away and then split into narrow strips. These were used to hold down small bundles of colorado grass, which were dipped in the red clay soil to form a thatch.

Alan and Roger split logs. One man stood at each end, and they worked in rhythm, each bringing his axe down or swinging it back up as his partner did the opposite. One morning Roger swung his axe, and it got stuck. Alan remembered: "The next swing was mine, and I came down toward Roger's head. As soon as I saw that his axe was stuck, and that he was in the way of my axe, I turned it so that the flat of the head came down on Roger's head. In the end there was not much damage done, but believe me, there were two weak and shocked brothers who went home right away and were put to rest for the balance of the day."

At long last the sisters and children piled onto the wagons for the drive up to Isla Margarita—those from Village 3 on April 9, and those from Village 2 on April 23. As they bumped through the forest, they admired the palm trees and the wide view of green meadows edged by dark woods. Finally they saw the thatched roofs of Primavera! "How beautiful it is!" Trautel thought. "Now we will shoulder the burdens together. Now all the tensions will be dissolved." There was Sekunda standing at a huge cauldron, stirring soup in a cloud of steam and smoke for their first meal together.

They lived in the Gallop Hut. It consisted of a corrugated iron roof on palm trunk supports. Four "halls" were still being built. These had thatched roofs on wooden posts sunk one meter into the ground. Neither the Gallop Hut nor the halls had walls to separate families. People used

The so-called Gallop Hut went up virtually overnight.

their luggage and mosquito nets to give an illusion of privacy and dressed before it got light. For the young people, this was part of the adventure; others needed to be encouraged to develop their sense of humor. "God wants the walls to fall!" Emmy quoted from a favorite hymn. Still, it was a trial for Irmgard and Anni. There was no time or place to mourn the loss of their little ones; Anni sometimes put her head under her pillow so that no one would hear her weeping.

Phyllis described their living conditions in a letter to her family in England:

> Sometimes we get very heavy dews in the mornings, and anything that is not under cover is very wet. As we have no walls to our houses, it penetrates everywhere. We have no furniture yet so live in our trunks, so to speak, and that is not too easy. When they have been packed tightly to come,

things don't go back so easily. It is a real camp life for us all. We all sleep on bedsteads but no mattresses, and when there aren't enough bedsteads, and there often haven't been, people sleep on benches. We are all hardening and it is good. Civilization has become too soft, and comfort takes too high a place in one's life to the detriment of one's inner life. I am very glad to have experienced the poverty and need of these first weeks in Paraguay. I had taken too much for granted in the old life before I came to the Bruderhof. I always thought I would have sheets to sleep in and bread and butter to eat, or at least margarine, and a cup of tea to drink. I never thought that I could eat rice for breakfast, rice for dinner, and rice for supper (and not made with fresh milk, only water and some cheap dried milk). We have little cow's milk, and that the children have. Bread is scarce, but we usually get a little once a day. Even so, I'm told we have better food than when the community was in Germany. I think that there they semi-starved.

Actually our chief difficulty is the sicknesses and having no doctor. So many (in fact, nearly all) our people and children have septic wounds on their legs and elsewhere. We are up against a very horrible kind of wound, such as one wouldn't meet in England. Nearly all the wounds have live worms or maggots in them and give much pain. Some of the children have these wounds in their heads and must have their heads shaved. My first experience with this nearly sapped all my courage and made me feel very sick, as I had to extract one from a tiny child's eye. I am nursing sick babies and children all day long.

◄┼►

When the group of 158 set out from England in February, they had left behind 70 men and women to negotiate the sale of the Cotswold Bruderhof and to work out the last passages to South America. But visitors continued to come and several asked to join. They found themselves in a quandary: should the entire Bruderhof movement leave Europe, or should they leave some behind to continue what they felt was work in God's harvest field? Philip Britts wrote in his journal:

> I thought, when our people left, that we should care no more for the offerings of England, and indeed, on that day, we heard and could see no birds except the Phoenix. But although we find that part of our hearts have gone across the sea, the handwork of God in England is still sweet. So is the task for God that Jesus has called us to take up. We long to be with our brothers who are in a land of blazing sun and flowers. But the chaste snowdrops comfort us, as do the modest English birds.

Again on March 11 he recorded:

> About 250 of our people have crossed the sea, in five voyages, in these desperate times, and not one has been lost. We can never be sufficiently thankful to God for this.
>
> Now we must seek to know what is his will for us who are still here. And on this day the Brotherhood will meet throughout the day, to seek together the answer to many questions.
>
> The position here is this: Many new people are still coming to us, more than ever before at this time of year. Our

Philip Britts, an English horticulturalist and poet who joined the community in the 1930s, died of a fungal disease in Paraguay, leaving his wife Joan and four children.

guest circle numbers about twenty. These things hold us to this country, but our brothers call to us from the new land:

"Position necessitates that you come soon. Help us to build Zion."

"Mission continues."

"Paraguay ripe for our message."

What shall we do? Shall we go or stay? Shall some go and some stay? How many shall go and how many shall stay? Who shall go and who shall stay?

And on March 13:

Today we received a cable from Paraguay. It contained good and cheering news: "Health good. Come immediately!" We felt that a direction had been pointed in our seeking. As we recalled the phrases that had kept recurring in the cables from the new land, we felt a great urge to take up this new task.

On April 23 the last group set out under the leadership
of Hardy's brother Heini, leaving behind three members
to finalize the sale of the Cotswold. (As it turned out, the
number of guests in England continued to increase daily.
In the end, instead of coming to Paraguay, those left behind stayed and began a new community, Wheathill.)

The final group included Ruth and Margaret, the doctors mentioned earlier, both of whom had just finished
medical school. Also in the group was Heini's sister Emy-
Margaret, who was dangerously ill with tuberculosis. Her
son Ben, seven, had been sick for months with pneumonia
and asthma.

The night before the group's departure, they met for
prayer and worship. Heini Arnold spoke:

> This evening we are looking towards the reunion with our
> brothers and sisters in South America. The most important
> task that has been given us is that there be established on the
> earth a people of God, a people of love and of unity. It will be
> wonderful when we are able to experience again a real com-
> munity, and also a real children's community, in a circle of
> 300-350 people. What we need for the future in America and
> for the small group which remains here is that God himself
> strengthens us. It is very important this evening and for the
> future that the will of Jesus Christ is before our eyes.
>
> When Jesus speaks of a city on a hill, he does not mean a
> religion of some kind. He really means a city from which the
> strength of God flows out. The character of this city becomes
> clear to us when we read the words of Jesus in his parting ad-
> dress to his disciples, in which above all, love and unity are
> emphasized.

Heini and
Annemarie
Arnold's children,
Roswith and
Johann Christoph,
on the Avila Star,
April 1941.

It seems quite impossible that a kingdom of peace might come among us humans, yet precisely this is what we ought to expect from God. We should expect the doors of heaven to open, so that the strength of God streams down and works among people. It will be accompanied by judgment, but it will bring the love of God. When we feel how great the need and the suffering of the world is, when we see great cities laid in ruins, and all the death and sorrow, it can bring us to despair unless we believe that God's love will ultimately triumph and rule everywhere.

We see in the prophetic words of Jesus that the closer love comes to the earth, the stronger is the hate and destruction that opposes it. It is into this struggle that we are now placed.

Wherever we may be, let us ask and expect and pray that God's love, strength, peace, justice, and righteousness might be revealed among us.

It is only in faith – faith that through judgment and suffering people draw nearer to God – that we can leave Europe tomorrow. We believe that there, in a new land, the building up of a city on a hill will be given anew.

The voyage went smoothly. On many evenings the group gathered, and Heini read to them words of expectation regarding the coming kingdom of God.

When they arrived in Buenos Aires, there was no one to meet them. But Hardy had written them a letter which was handed to them on the ship:

> Beloved brothers and sisters who now at last have crossed over the dangerous battlefield of the Atlantic Ocean!
>
> We greet you on your arrival in Buenos Aires with this letter instead of in person and are immensely glad about your coming. What a marvelous occasion it was when you told us that you had permission for the emigration of the twenty newest members after all. We could hardly grasp it. For although we have complete courage and faith, yet we felt increasingly that the only solution in this time is the gathering of the church.
>
> We are all united here now on a rolling hill, wonderfully situated and covered with palms and other beautiful trees, with the lovely name of Isla Margarita. The building up has already begun. A little group is on the former farm of the Primavera estate about three kilometers from here, called Casa Loma Hoby, to carry on the cattle farming and forestry

Susi Fros with two
of her children, Irene
and Jan Peter.

there. Cyril and Jan and Susi are still in the Chaco. But we expect them back from there any day. When we left the Chaco
early in March, we left our doctor and pharmacist behind
on the urgent request of the Mennonites, who are severely
troubled by illnesses. We did this in the faith and trust that
Margaret Stern would be coming with the next group. We
later regretted this very deeply, since a bad epidemic of dys-
entery which broke out among our own youngest children
has given us serious trouble. To our great pain, two of the
smallest and dearest little children have already succumbed
to it and been taken from us: that is, Daniel Keiderling and
Giovanni Mathis. Two babies are at the moment still in real
danger. We naturally called Cyril back by telegram, but the

way it is here, a telegram takes two weeks to get to the Chaco, and so far Cyril and Jan and Susi haven't arrived yet.

In regard to our health, apart from the malaria, which comes from the Chaco and is in general receding, we are plagued by severe conjunctivitis – eyes infected with pus – and many people have pus-filled ulcers on their legs, a very widespread phenomenon that is attributed to the change of climate. Moni and a few other sisters have to treat 135-150 pairs of eyes daily, and besides this, they often have to dress 124 wounds with bandages each day. So the doctors in your group will have lots to do.

You will surely have wondered why we called you away so urgently. We did this out of our sense that the situation in Europe is worsening to such a degree that a voyage across the sea would soon be impossible.

Hardy went on to describe the financial situation and other problems that had arisen.

The community was scattered in four or five Mennonite villages and in Primavera, in need of inner leadership and encouragement, and for weeks I had to ride around daily to take care of everyone properly. It was beyond my strength, and I could not give the community what it needed. You can hardly imagine the longing and ardent love with which we are awaiting you. It was especially difficult when the two little children died; often I had to be at a different place during their severe illness and once almost came too late to stand by the parents.

Mama [Emmy], Edith, and I plan to meet you in Asunción and travel the last, most difficult leg of the journey with you.

The accommodations here are extremely primitive. But by your arrival a little hut will be prepared for Emy-Margaret. We all live together in mass quarters in two or three large "halls," while a few sleep in tents. Providing food is not a simple matter either, because we lack money, and transportation and purchasing are so difficult.

In all the hardships I am describing, we have fought through to a courageous unity that has led or will lead to an important renewal. We feel that God wants to test and prove us in our faith through affliction and need, through poverty and difficulties of all kinds, and that all the more it depends on our being so firmly joined together in all needs that the great, mighty experience we expect at Pentecost from God will come about as purification and uniting in love and joy, a pouring in of the eternal light for the whole world. So we look forward immensely to your working, struggling, conquering, and carrying together with us in all inner, financial, and practical things.

We embrace you all in great love and joy and with the greeting of unity and peace,

Your lowly brother and sister, Hardy and Edith

⊰⊹⊱

Cyril Davies had stayed in the Chaco, where he worked as a doctor in the hospital in Filadelfia. Jan and Susi Fros with their two little children were with him; Jan was a trained pharmacist, and Susi helped translate for the Mennonites, as Cyril knew no German. Margrit Meier had also stayed behind. Her daughter, Lydia, was born on March 8, just a few days after everyone had left. Jan, Susi, and Margrit reestablished themselves in two neighboring houses. Susi cooked and washed for them and sewed diapers for Margrit's baby. She even managed to bake a cake to celebrate the new arrival and to encourage them all. Jan was able to earn some additional money giving violin lessons.

On April 17, a week after Giovanni's death, they received a telegram from Primavera: *"Segundo niño murió martes venid immediatemente para ayudar. Lucas veinte treinta y ocho."* ("Second child died on Tuesday, come immediately to help. Luke 20:38.") However, they did not understand the Spanish. Had Sekunda's unborn child died, and was she in mortal danger? Jan, Susi, and Margrit looked at each other. "The church is calling. We must go," Susi said. Jan went over to the hospital to tell Cyril.

At the hospital, however, there were two patients (an old man and a young woman) whom Cyril had just operated on, and both were in critical condition. The nurse was shocked at the idea of him leaving—how was she to care for them? The old man's brother was angry, too, and threatening. Cyril agreed that as doctor he could not leave without knowing more about Sekunda's illness, and without the brotherhood understanding the situation in Filadelfia. So, with heavy hearts, they composed a telegram explaining the situation and asking advice. Eagerly they waited for an answer. The next day there was no word, nor the next. Never had they felt so far away and alone. The young woman died, and the old man slowly improved, yet Cyril still felt he could not leave. Ten days later they wrote a

Cyril Davies, the Bruderhof's sole physician during the first hard months in Paraguay.

letter, signed by all four of them, explaining their position in detail.

> How are you all, especially Sekunda? We are interceding for her, that God may protect her; we long so much to hear how she is doing. It is now one and a half weeks since we received your telegram, and we haven't heard from you since. Did you receive our telegram? It is very hard for us that we are not able to travel and also that we have had no word from you as to what we should do. How terrible it is to be so far away! The whole time we feel a heaviness since we sent the telegram and we don't know what you think about it.

Evidently, the telegram never arrived. In the end, they

joined the others in Primavera as scheduled in early May. Hardly had they arrived, than Cyril had a new epidemic on his hands: trachoma, a potentially blinding eye disease common among the Mennonites, which they had hoped to protect the children from. Examining everyone, he found that two-thirds of the children and several adults had the dreaded disease. This was a heavy blow, for the only means of fighting it was to isolate those who were infected. Thus the Gallop Hut became, instead of a home, an isolation ward for children with trachoma. The infected babies were housed in another little hut. Marianne wrote, "Hard as it is to be separated from our children, no price is too high to save their eyes. If we think what the Mennonites suffered, or much more, if we think of the ever increasing misery caused by the war, then what we are facing is not much." But it tore at her heart when her three-year-old daughter told her father, "We don't have a Mama anymore."

Phyllis gave graphic descriptions of the various plagues in a letter to her family, written May 16:

> At the moment we have a big fight against the eye sickness. Many of our children and some grown-ups have been afflicted with it. Last week our doctor arrived from the Chaco. It was good that he came, we had so much illness amongst us and abscesses that needed a surgeon's knife. Also he could examine all the children's eyes and others, and it was a very terrible shock when he diagnosed trachoma (a very serious and dangerous eye disease which once originated in Egypt and has been wiped out of all European countries). Eighty-five children have it and five grown-ups. It is very contagious

and has meant isolation. This has been a difficult problem for us when we haven't any houses with walls. We have managed it as best we can. It has meant separation for many families. The treatment of so many eyes is a great work, and one needs a terrific amount of cotton wool or white rags for cleansing the eyes (also needed for the multitudinous sores and wounds on everyone). We daren't think of the time when our supply is at an end, which will be quite soon. We are going to experiment with the raw cotton which we can buy very cheaply, but it must be treated somehow before using. Our doctor works from morning till night unceasingly. The Mennonites come from far and near now they hear we have a doctor. Soon when the group arrives from England, we shall have two more doctors, and it will be easier.

The children are really very good with it all. They take it all as a matter of course, though the little ones cry very much when their eyes are treated. It is a very trying ordeal even for the grown-ups. Sand fleas getting into one's feet and burying themselves under one's skin and laying eggs is a great nuisance, but one of the lesser evils. They must be extracted as soon as one finds them, otherwise it could lead to abscesses. Nearly everybody has from one to three or four every day to remove. So far I've had only three altogether, so I'm lucky. I wear boots all the time, boys' boots, and I find them a great boon. Many people go barefoot, but I prefer not—as yet. We have built proper little places for men and women to wash in and have a spray bath. Those and the lavatories were the first to be built, and every day we bathe, children and all, so that although our conditions are primitive, we adhere strictly to cleanliness.

The arrival of the last large group from England at Primavera, May 29, 1941.

In addition to the sand fleas there were *uras*, worms that bored under the skin. The skin would swell, leaving an air hole for the worm to breathe through. A friendly Paraguayan took pity on the children suffering from these. He cut a piece of tobacco leaf, spat on it, stuck it over the place where the *ura* was, and told the child to leave it for a time. Without air, the *ura* died, and he came back and painlessly squeezed it out.

Emmy planned a children's festival to welcome the newest group from England and to cheer up the sick children. She organized the mothers to make dolls and other little toys. This helped make the enforced separation of parents and isolated children easier, and gave the children something to look forward to.

After Herr Rutenberg moved out of his house at Loma Hoby, a few miles from Isla Margarita, a group of sisters went to clean it, and then two families moved in. Loma Hoby was the headquarters of the estancia, and the new residents' main job was to look after the milking herd. The house had three rooms, and the families occupied two of them. The third was filled with boxes containing the community's library.

⊰⊹⊱

Three brothers and several Mennonite wagons were sent down to Rosario to meet the new arrivals from England. It was the end of May, rainy weather and growing colder by the day. Back in Primavera, everyone froze in their wall-less shelters, and mothers worried about their children. The next day the weather cleared and the wind died down. In the evening word went around: the first few travelers are at the gate! The children ran to meet them. Wolfgang poured petroleum on a huge pile of wood and set it alight – a welcome bonfire. What excitement there was! That night Heini kept everyone entertained with stories of the last months in England. He was a great storyteller with a sense of humor.

The next day, last-minute preparations were completed for the rest of the group, which was still on the way. Just as lunch was finished the wagons rolled up, one after another. The palms shone in the sun, and on the highest point of the property, the new thatched halls stood out against the

Food preparation in Primavera. The women (L to R) Elizabeth Watkins, Nona Mathis, and Nellie Dorell are peeling mandioca. Note the use of ship's luggage for seating.

blue. Trudi Hüssy, one of the newcomers from England, described her first impressions:

> As we drove over the yellow camp land, delicate daisies trembled in the wind. Then through a woods, and now the community appeared! Four huge straw roofs over large halls. Everyone ran to meet us. Oh, how our hearts burst within us. Those who had been in the Chaco looked pale and strained, with mended clothes. And the children! Their eyes were covered in black ointment, and mosquito nets hung from their straw hats. Where were their rosy cheeks and sparkling eyes? We heard the sad story of the deaths of Daniel and Giovanni and the serious illness of so many others. Our own trials seemed very small.

They spent the afternoon settling in, and in the evening they celebrated with a welcome dinner under the high trees. There was even dessert: Werner, the baker, had made 150 cakes over four days in a small underground oven.

The celebrating continued at every opportunity through Pentecost, with the children's festival and songs of thanksgiving. To end the long, happy Sunday, every child was given a paper lantern with a burning candle. The whole community walked in a procession around the buildings where the sick lay; and afterward they gathered for singing and hot punch. Brothers and sisters reminded one another of their vision for the future. Marianne recorded in her journal:

> We have now been here for a good month, in Primavera, at Isla Margarita, the highest point, more or less in the middle of our property. Day by day it becomes more of a "Bruderhof." There are many palms up here, signs of the peace of the city on the hill that is to arise here. May it truly become a fortress of Zion! God has led us into a beautiful land.
>
> In every respect this is a unique and wonderful time, where besides the joy and strain of building, the church will have to be newly founded inwardly. I have yearned for a long time that for once everything in the church might become new, like at the beginning, through a refreshing spirit, a Pentecost that will make us all new from the bottom up. God has led his weak, little flock together in such a wonderful way, one group after the other.
>
> But it becomes ever clearer to me that this will be given to us only insofar as we accept the way of Christ. We will have

to suffer and will be allowed to suffer; we must surrender and will be allowed to surrender ourselves completely; we shall pass through death, believing and expecting that the kingdom of God is near.

10

CHRISTINE

Not in fear and desperation,
But in stubborn, silent protest,
In the earth we laid our baby:
All the calm and tragic mothers,
All the brokenhearted maidens,
All the solemn-visaged brothers;
And we heaped the earth upon her
In a stubborn, silent protest.

Presently we turned and left her,
Lonely on the forest margin,
Turned and went once more to combat
With the Prince of Death and Darkness —
Not as they whose cause is hopeless,
But in certain expectation,
Fighting on towards the kingdom
And the overthrow of evil.

PHILIP BRITTS

BY JUNE, 329 men, women, and children had made it
across the ocean. Seven babies had been born since leaving

The first laundry in Isla Margarita, "isle of daisies."

England, and two had died. Finally all were together in one location. Would they be able to realize their dream of making Primavera a "city on a hill"? They knew it would take hard physical work; perhaps they did not realize that the spiritual work would be even harder. Phyllis wrote:

> We must wrestle with mother earth for our needs. Everything we must do ourselves, make our own bricks, lay our own pipes for the sewage system, and by and by weave our own cotton I expect. It is a very great experience to see the building up of a dwelling place for such a big community on land that is virgin, and every piece of wood to be taken from the trees. Our benches and tables all had to be hewn from our trees. Yes, we have a colossal work before us outwardly and inwardly.

Nina Wright had arrived in the final group with her husband, Wilfred. She described life in a letter to her family:

> We are quite well and agreeably surprised to find compara-

tively no mosquitoes at the moment, no snakes visible except in the plowed fields and an odd one in the forest, and no scorpions in our shoes in the morning or ants in our trunks! In fact we are very pleased to find ourselves so normal in a country so abounding in natural enemies. Only the eyes of the jaguars have been seen, and only the bark of the maned wolves has been heard, and the monkeys are almost invisible. We see vultures hovering in a wonderful fashion over the camp and are delighted to hear some rather lovely notes from a few birds in contrast to the parrots.

Mennonites and Paraguayans are here constantly to see our doctors as there are none in the neighborhood. The Mennonites are pale and sallow and poor and come in light wagons, and the Paraguayans come on horses, in scarlet blankets, barefoot with dark, sallow faces and also poor. They pay their bills in goods, the Paraguayan carretas (wagons with huge wheels) drawn by oxen bringing loads of mandioca and maize.

The police commissar of this district, Paraguayan, stole a cow and calf from our land and when arrested tried to make a breakaway and shot at his captors, who retaliated by shooting and wounding him. He now lies recovering and may at some future date return to power as shooting appears quite a common event.

A Paraguayan mother brought a child, wrongly treated in Asunción for some venereal disease. The child died here, and the despair of the mother expressed in terrible screams showed the terror of their life without God and their need for our help.

The Paraguayans are marvelous cowboys. By lasso they can catch cattle by their horns and one hind leg and fling

Nina Wright with
her son Gareth,
Primavera, 1943.

them to the ground for branding or worm extraction. One
of our brothers was nearly killed the other day. There was
a bull roped for killing, and Wilhelm went to remove the
rope where it had caught on an anthill (huge things). In the
process the rope slackened, and the bull charged and missed
Wilhelm, but caught the belly of the horse and slit it. Imagine Ruth Land sitting by the horse and putting back its guts
and sewing it up! But the poor horse died. One of our best
riders! (The children ride the horses bareback and are quite
fearless.)

A Paraguayan, when asked if he was married, said no, but he
had a concubine. Polygamy was made legal after the Bolivia-
Paraguay war, when nearly all the men were killed. We are

learning much about this country from these people, who are really simple and childlike. We are learning Spanish.

A laundry was set up near the well, about a quarter mile from the dwelling place. Meals were eaten outside under the trees when the weather was fair. When it rained, well, that was another story. Food was plain. It consisted chiefly of mandioca, a native, starchy root vegetable new to the Europeans. In addition there was rice and sometimes meat. Bread was scarce, and milk and eggs were kept for the mothers and children. Oranges and bananas made up for the lack of vegetables.

One day a large snake was found by one of the beds in the Gallop Hut, causing great alarm – and then great excitement among the children, when it was killed with a spade.

Fritz had managed to buy rolls of canvas, about a meter wide, and this was used around the outer perimeter of the halls to give a little protection from the wind, rain, and violent sandstorms. It was late fall now, colder than anyone had expected in the tropics.

In an island of trees, soon known as the "School Wood," the children helped their fathers build a thatched hut for use as a classroom. In time the underbrush was cleared, and a climbing frame and "giant stride" (a sort of merry-go-round) were built.

By the end of June, a small enclosed maternity house with a thatched roof – and best of all, three private rooms with doors! – had gone up too. Two babies were born there in early July.

Christine Kleiner with her siblings in England, 1940.

Around that time Fritz and Sekunda Kleiner's youngest child Christine became ill with a bad cough. She was just one and a half years old and had always seemed a little frail. Christine was one of many who had had malaria in the Chaco, but she had recovered and seemed to be doing well. Her cheeks were round and she was walking by herself. Then she got trachoma and was put in the isolation hut. Now she was breathing hard and kept trying to stand up at night. The sisters stretched wet sheets around her bed. On Monday, she was moved into one of the few real huts—her tiny arms tight around her father's neck and in one hand a doll her big sister had given her at the festival. Her breathing grew more and more difficult. Cyril examined her. Her throat was swollen and there seemed to be a horrible coating on her tonsils. Was it diphtheria? Should all the other children be inoculated?

Christine's breathing became worse, with attacks of choking. Cyril suggested a tracheotomy. Emmy, Moni, and the other medical staff spoke about the risk, but they knew of no other help. During the operation, the whole community gathered. Heini read from James 5:14–15: "Is any among you sick? Let him call for the elders of the church, and let them pray over him, anointing him with oil in the name of the Lord; and the prayer of faith will save the sick man, and the Lord will raise him up." Emmy held the child's limbs firmly. Suddenly she stopped breathing, and they could find no pulse. Emmy went out and spoke with Sekunda, and then left the hut to speak to the gathered community. She told them what had happened and urged them to intense prayer. In the meantime, Ruth tried to resuscitate the little one. All at once the child started to breathe again. A cry of joy broke out among those watching. She had overcome the first collapse.

Moni planned to spend the night with Christine. Everyone else disinfected the room and themselves, thankful and confident that God would restore the little girl. Moni wrote:

I took over Christine's watch around 11:00 P.M. She had fallen into quite a peaceful sleep. She breathed regularly, somewhat rapidly. Heini and Cyril came in around midnight. Both were happy that she was sleeping. "What a difference," Cyril said.

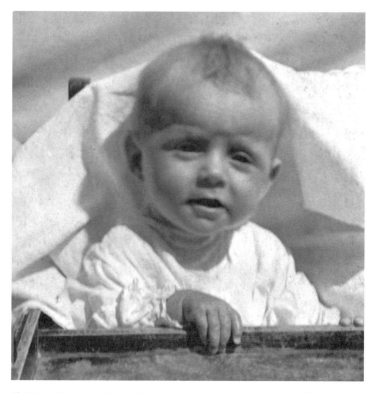

Christine Kleiner, who battled malaria, trachoma, and a fatal bout of croup – all
before the age of two.

Half an hour later she awoke quite happily. She seemed to
have no pain. She opened her little mouth for something to
drink. I gave her many spoonfuls of warm milk. Then she sat
up, stretched out her little arms to me and wanted to climb
out of her cot. I took her out. She was pleased. She picked up
the cup from the table and drank. She repeatedly stretched
out her little arms as if she wanted to fly. I sent for Cyril because she was growing so restless. When he came she was
lying in her cot again and sleeping.

She was breathing very rapidly. After a short while she

woke up with a radiant little face and pointed to the cup. Again she drank very well. Then she repeated the same movements. I took her out of bed again. She laid her head against me as if she wanted to sleep. Then she grew restless again. Her breathing was so rapid. The night watchman, Roger, came by and asked if I need anything. Her breathing was slowing down. I counted: 84 – 52 – 48! Suddenly the child's color changed, and she grew quite white. "Roger, come quickly!" I called into the night. "Wake Sekunda and Fritz, Emmy, Heini, and the doctors!"

I tried to help her breathing. When Cyril came she breathed deeply several times. Her parents and the others came in and stood with us around her cot. It was 2:30 A.M. when her little soul flew up to heaven.

Once more God had spoken. Edith wrote:

Sekunda and Fritz are very courageous. It's so shaking to see this mother losing her youngest child just when she expects another baby any day. Seeing death and life so close together is a contrast that the heart can barely grasp. Sekunda is pondering the thought and the longing that something more of eternity might permeate our daily life, that we might be truly expectant.

Christine died on June 25. (It had not been diphtheria, but croup.) She was laid out in a tent in the meadow, in a light blue gown embroidered with cowslips. After the strain of the previous day, she was now at peace. As brothers and sisters took turns at her side they considered the finality of death and their desperate situation here in the jungle.

Hans-Hermann and Fritz rode to Itacurubi to get the burial permit. The community had a short supper and then met in the dining room for the funeral. At the back stood the coffin with seven white candles in front of it. Heini read the Beatitudes and a few passages about Jesus' love for children. Then four brothers led the way with the candles, followed by the coffin and then twenty-four small candles, a long procession up to the burial ground. Hearts were heavy as the little box was slowly lowered into the earth. In the distance, a maned wolf howled.

When everybody returned there was mulled wine and sandwiches. It was the coldest time of year, and it felt like Christmas. Fritz shared memories of his daughter. They had taken her into the woods the previous Sunday, and the little girl had kept running, falling, and getting up again. "This is a picture of how we should be," Fritz said. "When we fall down in our weakness, we must not be discouraged, but ought to get up again and continue on toward our goal."

◄─►

On July 10, Sekunda gave birth to another little girl. Her arrival was a joy and encouragement to her bereaved parents. They named her Emmi-Christa, in memory of Christine. Tragically this child was to die as well, just before her first birthday.

11

BUILDING UP

Oh, come and share our weariness,
  the sweating of our toil!
  (Work clean, my hoe!)
Come, help to build a city
  that is rooted in the soil!
  (Gladly bend low!)
Cut down your proud ambitions,
  all your miseries and fears,
Oh, come and share our poverty,
  the laughter, and the tears.
  (Bend low, eternally bend low!)

JOHN RIDLEY BROWN

SLOWLY THE CHILDREN with trachoma were improving. Cyril examined them every two weeks. Mothers waited anxiously for the results and breathed with relief when they were declared clear. At the same time, other children were afflicted with breathing difficulties. It was soon apparent that what they had was more than a cold: it was whooping cough, and the virus had come with the last group from the ship. Heini and Annemarie Arnold's two little children, Roswith and Christoph, were very sick, and Christoph was only seven months old. In addition, several adults were in bed with streptococcus infections.

Adequate housing was a serious problem, as the only protection against disease was isolation. Still they managed to house afflicted children separately from those with trachoma. The strain was tremendous. After spending the day cooking and washing and tending the sick, women had to take turns doing night duty. Fathers meanwhile worked feverishly to improve housing. The men had started making clay bricks, so that they would be able to construct sturdier buildings. In addition, land was being cleared for gardening. Mothers and fathers longed to gather their children and establish family life, but this was impossible.

The medical staff did their best in the impossible conditions. Cyril drew blood from one of the children who had recovered from whooping cough and made a serum with which he inoculated all the other children. But like Ruth and Margaret, he was fresh out of medical school and had very little experience. None of the three were full members as yet—they would be baptized (and thus welcomed as full members) the following year—yet conditions forced them to take tremendous inner as well as medical responsibility. And they were expected to tend not only to Primavera's sick, but also to the local Paraguayans and Mennonites who came to be seen each day.

On July 10 Hans-Hermann reported:

1) Malaria: All 150 children have been tested. Of these, thirty-two tested positive, and of those who have recovered, many are still anemic. Many of the Chaco children are malaria-free.

2) Trachoma: More testing next week. No new cases so far.

3) Whooping cough: Still a lot of it, but no new cases. Isolation is so difficult that all children have to be inoculated. Christoph Arnold has an especially bad case.

4) Strep throat: Still around, particularly with Trautel Dreher, who is seriously ill. She also has bad skin trouble, which may be erysipelas.

5) Tropical leg sores have generally improved.

Around the same time Edith wrote to Hardy, who was on business in Asunción:

Primavera's first nursery—an open air cluster of cribs with mosquito netting.

Some parents have their children in four different places: one isolated with whooping cough in the third dwelling house; one with eye disease; one with those who have recovered from the eye disease but aren't allowed to have contact with whooping cough; and another one who is well. For several evenings in a row we have been reading the First Letter to the Corinthians, which ends with that wonderful passage about the resurrection of the dead.

What you write about the more tender emotional values in our community is very important, I think. It seems to me that the material and intellectual sides of life play an important role among us, but the emotional, which is more fragile, is not given sufficient spiritual value. You can't say it is not there at all, but it too easily gets separated and becomes mere sentimentality. Yet when the emotional sphere is filled by the Spirit, it is a particularly fine part of God's creation. God's world is so rich: there are angels and men and many spiritual worlds, the earth, the stars, the world of light and sound. Everything has its place in the wholeness of creation, as it says in First Corinthians: "There are heavenly bodies and earthly bodies; and the splendor of the heavenly bodies is one thing, the splendor of the earthly, another. The sun has a splendor of its own, the moon another splendor, and the stars another, for star differs from star in brightness" (1 Cor. 15:40–41). Each person, too, is a unique creation and has beauty that we can see with the eyes of the Spirit, shining through the coarser form and striving toward redemption. That is why we love people and why each life is holy to us: children, brothers and sisters, and everybody. I think there is something in all things that cries out for redemption, not only in human beings. Therefore everything we do toward building up is holy. Still, we mustn't fall into the superficiality that I feel sometimes when someone says, "We must do such and such—it's for the community." Of course that is correct, but I mean this differently, the way it is expressed in the words, "Lift the stone, and I am there."* We should live in constant awareness of the divine in everything we deal with. This is what gives life to our deeds and existence.

This land has a unique effect on me; it works somewhat like wine. I love Paraguay very much: its stark contrasts between hot and cold, between luxuriant beauty, almost like Paradise, and the hideous insects. Nothing here is tepid, and that is what I like. The starry sky, too, is wonderful. Let's enjoy God's creation together in its glorious oneness. This unity, the goal of creation, must be something marvelous. We have been able to catch glimpses of it now and then. What a grace from God it is to be called to recognize God's will and to feel his love.

Sylvia, a widowed mother with a four-year-old daughter, Clare, felt the same in her desire to follow God's will. When Clare developed whooping cough and then appendicitis as well, the brotherhood was called together to consider whether she should be operated on in her critical condition. Sylvia, sitting at her bedside, felt strongly the presence of God. She told Emmy that she wanted to depend on God and not on surgery. "In such a case," Emmy said, "the mother's feeling should be listened to." The brotherhood decided not to operate but prayed for healing—and the girl

---

*It seems she is referring to a well-known verse in the Gospel of Thomas: "Cleave the wood, and I am there; lift up the stone, and you shall find me" – "me" being Jesus.

did get better again. Later her mother said, "I remember sitting with Clare, feeling a wave of love and healing coming from the meeting, and how she began to take interest in things again from that moment on. In those critical days I learned the song, 'Our mighty healer now draws near.' How truly it expressed what we were experiencing!"

Phyllis wrote:

> Our fight against sickness is and will be a very great fight. This life demands our whole strength of heart, mind, and body. Sometimes I can hardly comprehend the fact that I have found this way of life. It is so wonderful a thing, and I could never, never depart from it unless I turned my back on Christ, and that is unthinkable.

The end of August meant the coming of spring. Nina described its unfamiliar beauty with an enthusiasm felt by many after the long, hard months of sickness, cold, and rain:

> Primavera means "springtime" and now we see signs of what we call spring. The lapacho trees are now mauve with blossom and shine out like jewels from all the woods—high up and trumpet-shaped. A yellow blossom is appearing all around too on other trees. Many trees suddenly have appeared in bright green after being a dull green. Some trees—the minority—have sprouted new leaves on their bare branches. Much of the thick high coarse camp grass has been burnt off and new, greener grass, still coarse, has appeared. Lovely little flowers of many varieties are always in the grass. At night from the wide camp a chorus—nay, a positive sym-

phony–arises on hot evenings from thousands of frogs. It begins during the day with the frogs that "chip-chip-chip" rapidly and continuously like sewing machines. These are accompanied by the gurglers at the same speed–"gug-gug-gug." Later the crying baby or Cockney cat frogs join in at the same and repeated interval without cessation–"meaw-meaw-meaw"; also at equal intervals but different from the babies, chorus the dog frogs "wough, wough, wough." The glowworms shine out like jewels, the fireflies flit like fairies, a night bird with strange cry flies over the frogs, and the maned wolves occasionally bark. The moon shines brilliantly, and now in springtime a strong scent of orange blossom is borne on the warm breeze.

Toward the end of August, the community had a special celebration. Nina wrote about it:

My duty was to help prepare breakfast, so I was wakened at 5:30 by the night watchman. I left Wilfred under the mosquito net and accompanied Marjorie and Sidney, who had also to help with the breakfast. We emerged from our dormitory into a beautiful but cold morning and passed the great, thatched, native-looking dwellings, crossed a narrow stretch of the big open plateau dotted with palms, sloping into a great expanse of camp (grassland) with oases of forest–and went into the temporary, corrugated-roofed kitchen with its three black cauldrons and brick stoves. I prepared buttered bread for various collections of children (whooping cough, etc.) plus parents. Alfred (the stores man) began to boil eggs for all the community, at least three hundred eggs. Wolfgang made us a delicious cup of coffee, in which we had a clot of

After months of using open fires, Primavera's cooks finally had a proper place to prepare food. By June 1941 they had more than 300 mouths to feed.

cream off the pan of milk – the first I've known here. Then he made coffee for all and maté for the children.

So at 7:30 we had breakfast, and at 8:30 almost the entire community were waiting by the pump on horse or wagon or foot to go through the camp to find a site for a second Bruderhof and corral for the milk herd. We were shown various possible sites for the same and discussed the situations. We saw land most of us had not seen before, and it really was thrilling, planning for the future and building up for tomorrow.

We ate grapefruits and nuts and sweets. We sang and the children played singing games, and some young ones danced folk dances in the bright sunshine. We ate in an open space in the little wood where we have all our meals in fine weather at long tables. We had a fruit soup thickened with mandioca flour – like tapioca, clear and sticky – and meat stew and mandioca and maté. Adolf Braun – beaming and very stout, with red beard and shining pink head – showed us a plan of Primavera. He told us of the Paraguayan who went to one forest spring to shoot an antelope from a camouflaged tree, and saw a jaguar. To his great horror another and another appeared to drink. The man stayed there trembling until they went away.

In the afternoon Wilfred and I were invited to coffee and cake in the long grass with Tom and Cecilia Paul and baby Emily. We discovered that Cecilia's mother had been a missionary in China, and that she had been born there and had gone to school in Japan. Really the amazing life stories behind people here!

We had supper at 7 o'clock and then a great and wonderful surprise – we went down to the industry shop, and there were seats and a screen and a projector, and we saw pictures of the Bruderhof first in Germany and then in England and even our arrival at Primavera from photographs. One photograph showed the edge of the grassy meadow over the deep valley with snow-capped mountains rising in front and a ring of children in the clear, brilliant sunshine. They seemed to be caught up in eternal youth and sunshine to remain forever poised in the glorious morning at the top of the world! A thrilling and wonderful picture!

Over the fall and winter, housing conditions slowly improved, and the men began drawing up plans for a hospital. In spring – September – a garden was planted. Eleanor wrote:

Sept. 1, 1941

We are working hard to build houses and workshops and a school and hospital for our large community and for neighboring natives who need so much the help of our doctors and nurses. At the same time we are plowing up stretches of virgin prairie land for garden and farm work and have already planted acres of grain, fruit, and vegetables. Until these are ripe we must live sparingly, but from April until September we have had a never-ending supply of wonderful oranges from an orange wood on our land and bananas from native plantations. Recently we have had hundreds of grapefruits given to us by natives in return for medical help. This week our first cabbages, peas, and carrots came to the table, and soon we shall have tomatoes. But a sadder feature of this land is the terrific heat, which is almost unbearable at times and the tremendous tropical storms, when wind, rain, thunder and lightening go mad together. June, July, and August are the coolest months, and the nights are really cold, although the midday sun is still very hot. We have recently had really frosty nights, and for us who are still in camping conditions, this means quite a trial of endurance.

Hand in hand with the agricultural work goes that of building, which in itself is only made possible by hard work in the forests, felling huge trees whose trunks are then brought in by teams of oxen to be prepared in our sawmill. We have quantities of good timber but little else for building. Before us is the tremendous programme of building up—dwelling houses, children's day houses, school, hospital, workshops, farm buildings.

And we are fired to this by the knowledge and fact that God has brought us here and has a great purpose for us in

Fathers and sons alike joined in to thatch a new roof.

Paraguay. The need of this war-tormented world has not been forgotten by us. It is here also. Even among these simple natives is much strife and sorrow and suffering – they too need the love of a life in Christian brotherhood, and gradually, in spite of language barriers, we are coming nearer to them. Besides the natives, there are numerous settlements of Europeans, and we hope to reach them, too. Our great longing is to build up a "city on a hill" – a place in which at all costs God alone reigns, and today the urgency of this is very real. At Christ's second coming, will there be those who, not having bent the knee to the princes and dictators of this world, will be ready to receive him? And in this time when men are gathering together in such masses to serve other "princes," we feel that we must use all that we have in full dedication to Christ and his kingdom.

October 9, 1941

It is so difficult to tell you all we would wish to of our life here. Its newness and its width and depth of experience is so terrific. The tropical winter is just over—cold nights and sometimes cold, often very warm days—and now the heat begins. The midday hours are unbearably hot, even to rest in, and tremendous thunderstorms are common. These are indescribable passion of nature—crashing thunder, powerful lightening tearing the sky, and great downpours of rain and hail. Sandstorms, but not (as in the Chaco) very severe, are also known. A strange, strange land of interminable plain and forest land, weird animal calls, especially during the night, rapid luxurious growth of all plants (especially weeds!), extremely simple homes and villages of the natives, and a storybook type of travel—such as ours. To see in the far distance a slow caravan of oxen wagons, ten foot high wheels, cylinder sort of roof, drawn by six oxen, goaded by clanging spike-goads and accompanied by horse riders, is commonplace now but nevertheless thrilling. These come to bring patients to our doctors, or to bring supplies of bananas or maize, etc., for us, because as yet we haven't our own produce. Almost all visitors come on horseback—men, women, and children. I've almost forgotten what cars look like!

12

REPENTANCE

I have cried in despair
To the skies at night:
God, who art there
In glory and light,
Check not thy hand,
Deal thy judgment to me,
Who so arrogant stands
And will hear not nor see.

PHILIP BRITTS

TRAUTEL DREHER was in bed for several weeks, unable to care for Felix or her other children. She was not the only adult who was sick. Heini Arnold was also in bed with the recurrence of an earlier illness. Annemarie was torn between caring for her husband and her baby, Christoph, who was still sick with whooping cough.

As the winter weeks drew on, the trachoma and whooping cough ran their courses. Slowly families were able to live together again. Trautel was able to get up and have her children around her. But the strain of the past months was

Heini and Annemarie Arnold with their children, early 1942.

showing. Underlying jealousies, some dating back months or even years, erupted in unfriendly comments. Any sense of adventure had dissipated in the face of hard reality, and most seemed to have lost sight of their vision.

Heini's condition worsened. He was lying in a little hut, suffering severe pain, weight loss, shortness of breath. Cyril thought he would die. At the end of September he rallied his strength in an effort to call everyone back to their "first love," to the initial joy and enthusiasm that had brought them to community, and to the vision of a new society that had inspired the first members, including his parents, Eberhard and Emmy, in 1920. On September 29 a letter he dictated was read aloud to the group:

> You beloved ones who are allowed to be actively at work on earth, your only commission from Jesus through the church is to work and be active for his kingdom, for his future rulership. There is nothing greater than when Jesus shall one day reign and rule over everything. It will be so wonderful that you and all others who take part will have your breath taken away for joy. And there is nothing greater on earth than to have worked for this kingdom.
>
> I am unworthy to write to you. But I believe God wants to give me strength. Be active! You may work today, tomorrow, as long as strength is given to you, for another ten years perhaps, or twenty, or even more. I wish I could spur you on to live intensely. Use the time for the kingdom. Love one another.
>
> My father said, "We have not yet come to true mission; to pray for it is ever more urgent." Beloved ones, I believe that God wills this for you for the sake of the kingdom, for the sake of the battle of the spirits. Pray for this mission, when you have found true repentance. To pray for mission is truly greater than to ask for such gifts as healing of the sick, etc., which are subordinate to mission. I believe that frequently we pray for what we want and think very little of what God wants at this particular time. I believe he often would hear us more quickly if our prayers were more directed to the will of God and our hearts were stimulated by the good Spirit, toward whatever God needs at this moment. We should not

The hut (left foreground) where Heini Arnold lay, deathly sick, in September–October 1941.

pray for what we would like to have for this day, but pray to be able to carry out what God wills.

Over the next days, the community gathered several times outside the hut where Heini was lying, too weak to get up and join them. Who knew how long this beloved teacher would live? Would the illnesses that had robbed them of babies now begin to take adult members as well? Rather than depress them, however, Heini's illness seemed to draw them together in a deeper bond, as described in a letter Nina Wright wrote to her family:

We have never doubted that it was God's will for us to join the community and consequent upon that to come to Paraguay. When we arrived we were greeted with real joy and love, but everything seemed to soon become subsidiary to a tremendous drive of hard practical work and the resulting tiredness. The illness seemed pretty appalling—almost ninety isolated for eyes and twenty-four for whooping cough, and tropical sores still oozing viciously from summer time, and sand fleas small but a nuisance, and a fair amount of uncomfortable heat—no quiet most of the time, and no privacy on the whole. All these disadvantages became more prominent because of no development of deep love and inspired friendship—on my part and obviously among others. Our "quiet times" had become crisis ones on the whole, and we were chiefly running on our own steam which made everything seem terribly hard. Then I realized that solitude with God must dominate and give power, or our life here had no significance and we were better in the past surroundings.

Last Sunday was one of the most outstanding days of my life. Heini was borne to us on a stretcher, apparently mortally ill, and in great agony he gave us a never-to-be-forgotten call to repentance, to come to Christ and the cross, and to God who would make all things new. He condemned specific sin and admitted his own sin. He had to be given stimulants all the time, and his breathing was often terrible. His voice was sometimes a whisper, and sometimes loud and irregular, and many times he was in great pain, but the power of Christ dominated him, and he was able to finish. Three days later he came again, and he was so ill that we thought he would die before our eyes. He expressed great love for us and Christ and said *good* men must repent. We have since then held ourselves ready night and day to come together to pray or sing for Heini. Many times we have gathered round his little house to help him to be victorious in his terrible struggle for Christ to be conqueror in life or death for him and in all of us in the community.

Some of Heini's words were recorded at the time:

The nearness of the kingdom of God cannot be measured in time. Jesus says: the kingdom is now near! And it was, paradoxical as it sounds, at that time nearer than now. It wasn't nearer in terms of time, but rather in terms of space. The kingdom of God has to be fought for and wrestled for.

When a person feels very big and fat in what *he* represents and what *he* says, that is democracy. We want to pray for Christ's rulership among us. When Christ doesn't rule, we are just a mass, whether a democracy or a dictatorship. But when Christ comes to his complete rulership among us, then we shall in the truest sense become brothers and sisters.

We want to be courageous. There are many who have suffered so courageously, like Anni, Irmgard, Sekunda, and many more. These women who have suffered and fought through so much are real examples for all the women in the church, because they somehow experienced, through the deaths of their children, the suffering of Christ.

We must never become lukewarm again; the hour is too serious. The kingdom of God can break in tomorrow, or even today. I could die tonight, and tomorrow we could be united in the kingdom of God.

It is something completely overpowering that already now eternity is very near us in the bond between this place and the church above. The stronger the connections are in the church with the eternal light, yes, with the cross, the nearer the kingdom of God will be to us. Perhaps it is not so much a matter of time, but of space. If Jesus Christ were to walk into this room to bless you all and to take me to him, then the kingdom of God would be very near, as near as it was when Jesus was on the earth.

But it will be something still different when the whole

Heini and
Annemarie
Arnold in
Primavera,
ca. 1942.

earth is conquered for the kingdom. We have to pray, to plead and wrestle for this kingdom, so that this earth, which is now ruled everywhere by Satan, can be re-won for God. When a new Bruderhof is founded, it is always so difficult for a piece of land to be completely freed from the rulership of Satan and won for the kingdom of God. It is the task of the church to demand that here on this piece of land everything belongs to God.

Live intensively in the expectation of the Lord! Each day is more than a day. It seems to me sometimes that a day is more like a year. I ask myself every evening now, have I really loved enough, hoped enough, fought enough, worked enough?

Listening outside his hut, brothers and sisters were moved by his words. They asked one another for forgiveness and determined to work for unity. Marianne wrote some weeks later:

> We haven't experienced such a time of struggle and the victory of Christ since Eberhard's time. And yet at the bottom of their hearts everyone longed for it, most of all for complete unity in the church.
>
> I had had the strong feeling for a long time, especially since we left England, that we needed such a clear separation, that at some point God would have to sweep away all our human garbage that had piled up over the years. When Heini was so seriously sick that medically speaking we expected his death any time, it was given to him to call everyone to repentance. Repentance really took place, and the brotherhood was newly founded. We all had to forgive one another so much. This is the message of the cross. Kurt and I also learned it anew; we thanked God again for the love and the way that was given to us both. By a miracle Heini overcame death and is now quietly recovering.

Nina wrote:

> The first tangible result of these meetings was that the older members confessed and asked forgiveness for having to a great extent become reliant on tradition over a period of years rather than on the living Spirit. This was a great joy to

all. A new love has been born amongst us, and the way of the cross is opening up for us.

I was spiritually dying for want of inspired love, and I sensed this terrible need in others. With this realization last week came a real horror of how I had strayed away from God's love, in which I had known such joy through Jesus Christ, and a real horror at my indifference to people's need here. I asked God to forgive me, and the people with whom I work. I am now determined to know nothing save Jesus Christ. I can work in unity only with those who are also so determined and will therefore listen to God perpetually and obey. I also have a great and glowing hope that we will allow all things to be made new!

13

FELIX

We have not come like Eastern kings,
With gifts upon the pommel lying.
Our hands are empty, and we came
Because we heard a baby crying.

We have not come like questing knights,
With fiery swords and banners flying.
We heard a call and hurried here –
The call was like a baby crying.

But we have come with open hearts
From places where the torch is dying.
We seek a manger and a cross
Because we heard a baby crying.

PHILIP BRITTS

IN OCTOBER, Trautel's little Felix seemed to be getting sick. He was eleven months old now. One evening when she went to pick him up from the nursery, he was lying in his crib, crying piteously. She was alarmed. He had a loud

Trautel Dreher
with her children.

cough, hard and barking. He seemed to have a fever, and his breathing was quick, with something of a rattle. The memory of little Christine suddenly flashed through her mind. Her breathing had been exactly the same.

It was a restless night. His breathing grew more and more rapid. His chest heaved, his eyes were dull; his arms stretched out listlessly on the blanket. His voice was hoarse when he cried, his lips parched.

The next day Felix was carried to the thatched house. Here it was quiet and airy. Through the long night Trautel sat at his side, determined to watch with him although she was still weak from her own illness. The night watchman came regularly with hot water. Trautel was thankful for his quiet support. She looked into her son's tortured face. His eyes were half open, and he could not sleep. Her heart was heavy with foreboding. She prayed, "God, do what you will with my Felix. I will be prepared, even if death should come." A great peace entered her heart. She opened her Bible and read of the raising of Lazarus.

The next morning, October 15, when his older brothers and sisters came to his bed, he opened his eyes wide with joy and tried to smile. They stood quietly. Felix looked at each one in turn and then half closed his eyes. The children went out quietly and sorrowfully. This was the last time they would see their little brother.

Moni, Emmy, and Hardy came in. The church met to pray for the child; it was a matter of life or death. His little face was paler; his lips fluttered rapidly. What was he trying to say? Then suddenly his eyes opened wide, and wider still, a heavenly blue. Then they glazed over. "Moni, he is dying!" Trautel cried.

Hardy said a prayer: "Lord, give him life, if it is thy will." The child took his last breaths, and died.

"Jesus, come!" cried Leo, the words wrung from his heart. Now Moni put Felix into Trautel's arms. Quietly, softly, his tiny soul had gone into eternity. Or had eternity come to those left behind? They felt such peace in the room.

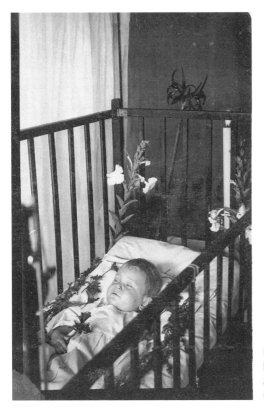

Felix Dreher, shown
here after his death
at eleven months in
October 1941.

Later Trautel wrote in her diary: "O my child, with what
pain I bore you! Is it joy or pain that now fills my heart and
bosom? I do no know. I only know that I give my child
back to God who gave him to me."

Moni put his little body back in the bed. It was as if he
were asleep. They gazed at him for a long, long time. It had
all happened so quickly. No lengthy illness – one hard day
and a still harder night – and now he was gone.

Alfred prepared a quiet room for him in the new baby
house. He lay in the little coffin a handful of men had made

for him. A red amaryllis with seven large blossoms was placed at his side.

The coffin was closed. Leo and Trautel stood next to it, tears streaming down their faces. A strong wind swept across the grassland as the community gathered under the starlit sky for the funeral, but the tall candle that Trautel carried continued to burn in spite of it. Georg spoke about the child's short life and about the victory of God's love over all doubt and self-torment. He had to raise his voice in order to be heard over the wind.

In a long procession the brothers and sisters walked out to the burial ground, the stars shining above them. Slowly the coffin was lowered into the earth.

14

CHRISTOPHER

From now on you will fear neither death nor the devil. You will walk through the suffering of this world, and your name will be Christopherus, which means "bearer of Christ." Your soul will be illuminated with the love of God, and you will show mercy to all people.

HANS THOMA

from The Legend of Christopherus

ON NOVEMBER 2, as the adults were eating dinner, the sister babysitting the youngest children checked on four-month-old Christopher Sumner, who was presumed sleeping in his crib, and found him cold and not breathing. She ran to call his parents and the medical staff out of the dining room, but nothing could be done.

Christopher had been born on July 2. His mother, Luise, had been carrying him at the time of the Atlantic crossing, and she had had some anxious moments on her arrival

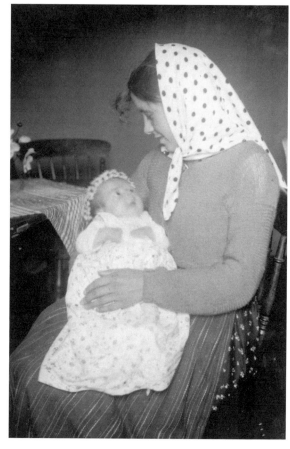

Luise Sumner (here with her daughter, Ursula, in England) later lost a son, Christopher, in Paraguay.

in Asunción. All the same, he had had a normal birth and seemed to have no serious health problems. On the night in question, his mother had nursed him and put him to bed, and neither she nor her husband, Bruce, had noticed anything unusual.

A fifth little grave was dug. Again the community gathered, solemn and bewildered. Following the burial, the brothers and sisters met, and Bruce spoke:

Tonight I want to speak for our son Christopher. Our position has been serious, and I believe it still is. But praise to God, the enemy has not had the power to take any of us except five small, innocent children. These the enemy took hold of with icy hand, but they have gone straight back to God because they were pure.

I know that many mothers are anxious in their hearts for their small ones. I know it because we have also been anxious. And this anxiety is a terrible thing. Mothers feel it much more than fathers, because they are much more closely bound to their children. I do not say we should not mourn; but we must understand that the pain is a personal pain, a pain because the child is not with us. If we think of Christ, it is only joy.

Heini spoke to us about our son an hour after he had died, and what he said has become very important to me: "Christopher has conquered, we not yet. He has overcome, we not yet. He is at the goal, we not yet."

And now five small children have died. All five have had immeasurably much to say to us, much more than we adults can say because we are not so pure or so loving. I am thankful to God that this little child, all five children, without one of them being able really to speak, can really say something for the reign of God and for God's cause. And as my son has been only a short time in this world, without being able to say what he had to say, I feel it my duty as father to try and put into words what he had to say.

Christopher was born on July 2. Through his birth, something broke into our family, like a beam of light from God. We called him Christopher and thought of him coming over the water with us. We hoped that when he became a man he would also be a Christopher, a bearer of Christ. For four

Bruce and Luise
Sumner.

months he was a true light of the sun, and on November 2,
between seven and eight in the evening—God alone knows
when—he died. He was quite alone in the darkness when the
evil one, who was the murderer from the beginning, came
and stretched out his cold hand and froze the little heart with
his touch.

Now little Christopher has really become, for me at least,
a "Christ bearer"—but not as I thought. I thought that he
would grow up, and that I as his father would try to bring

him to Christ, in the hope that he would witness to Christ. But it has not been so. I have only just recognized that from his very birth he was a bearer of Christ. Ultimately children are greater bearers of Christ than we; they show much more of Christ than many of us who can talk so much.

It has been said that "Love is joy in others." Christopher was a child of joy. He never asked when anyone came to him, "What kind of man is that? With what sin is he laden? Is he bitter, moral, cold, or proud?" He looked upon a person's face, and he was joyful, and he usually laughed. I have sometimes looked at my three small children and thought, "If you knew what kind of a man you have for a father!" And I have been ashamed, and yet at the same time I was glad that they did not know. Christopher especially loved his dear mother, and he greeted her with special happiness and laughter. We are all brothers and sisters, and you know how weak my Luise is, but he never asked, "What kind of mother do I have?" He loved her more than anyone in the whole world. His love was unclouded.

I have been stirred and moved, really to love all. If we take this message to heart I think our hearts will break down.

15

CHRISTMAS

Take heart, the journey's ended:
I see the twinkling lights,
Where we shall be befriended
on this the night of nights.
Now praise the Lord that led us
so safe unto the town,
Where men will feed and bed us,
and I can lay me down.

ELEANOR FARJEON

CHRISTMAS was a time of celebration. The group had survived the first and most difficult year. They had come safely across the treacherous ocean and passed through the inhospitable Chaco. Five little ones had been lost, but the group was together, determined to face the coming year with faith and courage.

The new year would begin with another infant death: Hardy's sister Monika had jaundice and her little girl was born prematurely. Later in the year, Fritz and Sekunda's Emmi-Christa would die after days of continuous vomit-

The Primavera burial ground (shown here in 1944). More than forty brothers, sisters, and children were buried here.

ing. Numerous inner and outer hardships lay ahead, unforeseen. But now it was time to pause and to give praise and thanks to God.

November 30 was the first Sunday of Advent. That morning the mothers and fathers brought to the service all the babies who had been born that year. There were fourteen who had been born since the last such meeting, which Hardy had held so many months ago in the Chaco – among them Lydia Meier, Avila Dyroff, Primavera Stevenson, and Emmi-Christa Kleiner. Moni's husband Georg Barth took the meeting:

> We will first think of the little babies taken from us: Daniel Keiderling, Giovanni Mathis, Christine Kleiner, Felix Dreher, and Christopher Sumner. In this morning hour when we have come together to present fourteen of our little ones to the church, we know ourselves one with these other little ones who have been called back to the place from which

Mothers and babies in the yard of Primavera's first nursery, ca. 1942. The women (L to R) are Sylvia Walker (later Beels), Elsbeth Friedrich, Winifred Pacey (later Hildel), Nancy Trapnell, and Liesel Arnold.

they came. The little children who are no longer among us were beams of light to us from eternity. They ignited flames among us and awakened joy in us. In their short time on earth they fulfilled the task for which they were created.

There is hardly a more fitting day than the first Sunday in Advent to bring these many children before the church. We expect the birth of Christ, the feast of the coming of the Child. The Christmas festival belongs completely to the Child.

We must think of the parents of the children. We wish for the dear mothers the humility of Mary, the loving, obedient mother. We wish that they might receive the childlike spirit which has come to them through their children. The souls of children are called from eternity. Fathers and mothers have a great responsibility to stand in reverence before the fact of becoming father and mother.

Each mother stood up with her baby and held it up for all

to see. The smallest ones were laid on a table in the middle
of the circle. Georg spoke again:

> In bringing their children to the church, the parents are say-
> ing that their children belong to the church and to God. In
> the prayer on their behalf, these children are entrusted and
> dedicated to God. Our life is a life that expects the future.
> The mother bears these little ones in expectation of the fu-
> ture, waiting for a true human being in the image of God
> to be born. Also in this expectation of the future, we give
> the child to God and to his church. Jesus took the little chil-
> dren into his heart. He embraced them and said, "Unless you
> become as little children, you cannot enter the kingdom of
> heaven." We ask that those of us who are grown up may be-
> come childlike, that we may be used for the building up of his
> kingdom. And we ask that God might care for and protect
> these little ones for the rest of their lives, from all danger to
> body, soul, and spirit, so that they might grow up to be used
> for the service of God and his kingdom.

‹‹-›-›-›

Over the next weeks, all thoughts were turned to Christmas
preparations, though it was—for a group that was almost
entirely from northern Europe—rather hard to imagine
Christmas in the heat of summer. The children worked
on a pageant. Instead of fir trees, mothers decorated their
"homes"—the large halls were now divided into private
quarters with blankets and curtains—with palm branches
and sunflowers. Hardy and Edith built a little wooden stable

with Christmas figures that Edith had made, and the children enjoyed dressing up as shepherds and angels. Shortly before Christmas, even Santa Claus found his way through the jungle! He arrived on a wagon drawn by horses – and found his costume unbearably hot! Brian Trapnell wrote:

> Imagine Christmas in scorching midsummer weather! The idea of it seemed strange to us too, but on consideration maybe certain advantages can be imagined for having it so. The work of preparation had been going on for some time. The sewing room had been especially busy making things: shirts for the men, blouses and new frocks for the women and children, etc. The shoemaker had the assistance of a Mennonite cobbler, making sandals and repairing shoes. For the last fortnight the sawmill and woodworking shops had been a hive of industry, making toys for the children, tables, benches, cupboards, etc. The bakers had been busy baking cakes and biscuits daily for a long time.
>
> At last the great day arrived, and the usual work stopped at midday on Christmas Eve, and we got ready for the celebrations. Following an early supper we went with the bigger children to a little nativity tableau and sang a few songs, and returned home, the children carrying lighted candles, which looked very beautiful in the gathering darkness. Here we found our presents all nicely set out. Our Peter was delighted with his array of gifts, especially his hobbyhorse, a little wagon filled with blocks, an old doll redressed as a Paraguayan cowboy. Mark too had various new articles of apparel, but he was too young to voice his appreciation of them! When the children had been put to bed, we had a meeting, followed by tea and cake, and later to bed!

Christmas morning we were quite free from any "official" meeting or anything, so breakfast was a very leisurely affair. Later a group of musicians from the neighborhood came, spotlessly dressed in white shirts and white trousers and soft black hats. They had a harp and two guitars and played a number of airs. They were native Paraguayans, and it was very nice of them to come. They were, of course, suitably rewarded with coffee and cakes. In the evening we had the children's nativity play in a realistic setting in the "School Wood," one of the small "islands" of forest. It was very good.

The following afternoon a group of thirty-five or so set off down to Friesland to give a performance of our Christmas play for the Mennonites. We went down in wagons and took luscious watermelons with us. It was very hot! We got down just before dusk and completed the preparations for the show, which was in front of the school in Village 2, where we had lived for a while soon after our arrival. The play was based on the parable of the wise and foolish virgins. I was in the chorus, and we sang three chorales set by Bach. Afterwards we were invited out to various households. I went with four others, and we had biscuits (homemade) and coffee with a Mennonite and his family in Village 5. They played some homemade guitars and mandolins. One was a typical, triangular shaped instrument. We also sang one or two carols. I am afraid we were all too tired to really appreciate the lovely ride back in the glorious moonlight! Home at 1:00 A.M. and so to bed!

So the first year in Paraguay came to an end. As Marianne wrote:

With great thankfulness we left the old year behind and began the new. In the past months God gave so much to the church that our hearts have not really taken it in. One thing stands above all else: God's love and grace and mercy are great and were with us also in the dark hours of death.

One evening shortly before, Fritz and Sekunda had dressed as Joseph and Mary and reenacted their search for lodging, singing an English Christmas carol. They walked from building to building; at each stood an "innkeeper" who refused them shelter. Finally they came to the barn.

Take heart, take heart, sweet Mary, the cattle are our friends:
Lie down, lie down, sweet Mary, for here the journey ends.
Now praise the Lord that found me this shelter in the town,
Where I with friends around me may lay my burden down.

As the men and women joined in the song, they could not but think of their own experiences as weary exiles over land and sea. Hadn't they too found a place to rest along the way?

◄‹··›►

Although the Bruderhof put down strong roots in Paraguay during its first years there—and although they would call this obscure, landlocked country home for the next two decades—their settlement there hardly represented the end of a journey. Over the next years, one difficulty after another would test their mettle. Outwardly, they struggled against innumerable obstacles as they built up a productive farm, a school, a hospital, and solid dwellings. Inwardly, they found themselves in an ongoing fight for love and unity and mutual forgiveness – for true community, as over against the sort of co-existence marked by legalism, bureaucracy, and majority rule.

It wasn't easy. Crises erupted, leaders rose and fell, and illness continued to plague not only the children, but adults as well. In 1943, Edith was unexpectedly snatched away, following a bout of appendicitis. Fritz succumbed to a fatal infection after an accident with a lathe in the community's turnery. Trautel died suddenly on her eldest daughter's 17th birthday, leaving a brood of motherless youngsters. Philip died of a rare fungal disease. There were others.

And yet throughout the community's darkest hours there flared up again and again the longing for something new – the longing to recapture that first love, which Heini had called the group to in late 1941, as he lay at death's door. We catch a glimpse of it from a letter written to him around that time from Sydney and Marjorie Hindley:

> In our meeting tonight a number of the brothers and sisters stressed the necessity of getting back to the Gospels – that Christ alone must be the center of our life, and that only from this center can we hope to return to the real joy and unity which God intends for his people. I myself feel that this is the only way. And I feel too that the significance of the cross must come much more clearly to expression in our daily lives. We must more clearly bear one another's burdens

Folk dancing at Primavera. Despite death and deprivation, the joy of building up a new community in a new land was never entirely quenched and leaves a lasting legacy.

and be much more ready to recognize our own responsibility. We are determined with our whole hearts to fight on.

No matter how many attacks they weathered from without, no matter how many human failings threatened to pull them down from within, this determination to fight on for the establishment of God's rule on earth—and their faith that he remained faithful and merciful, despite periods of judgment—held the group together and saw them through their hardest trials. The fact that we, their grandchildren and great-grandchildren, are still living in community today, more than half a century later, is surely a testimony to their legacy.

APPENDIX 1
*Transatlantic Crossings of Bruderhof Travelers
(England to South America), 1940–1941*

AUGUST 1, 1940
2 on the Scythia *to New York*

Johnson, Guy

Meier, Hans

NOVEMBER 24, 1940
81 on the Andalucia Star

Arnold, Emmy

Arnold, Hans-Hermann and Gertrud, Rose Marie, Franzhard

Arnold, Hardy and Edith, Eberhard Claus, Johannes, Gabriel,
Mirjam

Bateman, Phyllis

Bolck, Heinz

Bolli, Dorli

Braun, Adolf and Martha, Elfriede

Davies, Cyril

Dreher, Leo and Trautel, Tobias, Magdalene, Eva, Martha, Josua,
Felix

Ecroyd, Maria

Fischer, Wilhelm and Lini, Lucrezia, Johanna

Fros, Hermann and Iet, Elske

Fros, Jan and Susi, Irene

Gneiting, Alfred and Gretel, Jakob, Michael, Dorothea,
Margaretha, Lienhard

Grimm, Hans

Hildel, Rudi

Hinde, John

Hollander, Walter von

Johnson, Eleanor, Timothy

Kleiner, Fritz and Sekunda, Susanna, Traindel, Matthias,
  Heinrich, Fritz, Christine
Meier, Margrit, Klaus, Andreas, Hans Jürg, Daniel, Verena,
  Hanna
Paul, Tom and Cecilia
Stevenson, Alan and Nellie
Wegner, Gerd and Gertrud
Wiegand, Gerhard and Waltraut, William, Annelene
Zimmermann, Kurt and Marianne, Renata, Mathilde, Emmy,
  Hans

JANUARY 12, 1941

6 on the Tuscan Star

Beels, Francis
Hundhammer, Karl
Kleine, Ludwig
Loewenthal, Wolfgang
Mettler, Artur
Wohlfahrt, Albert

FEBRUARY 7, 1941

159 on the Avila Star

Allain, Roger and Norah, Paul, André
Arnold, Hermann and Liesel, Clara
Arnold, Käthe
Barron, Harry and Edith
Barth, Georg and Moni, Jörg, Klaus, Stephan
Bennett, Walter
Berger, Charlotte
Boller, Hannes and Else, Lisbeth, Hans Uli, Christoph, Elias,
  Dorothea
Braun, Walter and Marei, Laurenz, Friedreich, Grace, Deborah
Caine, Michael
Cheney, Howard

Dorell, Gerald and Nellie, Roy
Dyroff, August and Freda, Martin, Paul, Bernhard, Avila
Ebner, Kathrin, Anna
Fischli, Migg and Hilde, Josef, Susanna, Gottlieb
Friedemann, Werner and Erna, Maria, Margarethe
Friedrich, Elsbeth
Friedrich, Hildegard
Fros, Gerrit and Cornelia
Goodwin, Fred and Margaret
Habakuk, Daniel
Habakuk, Johannes
Halliwell, George
Harries, Llewelyn and Bessie, Jennifer, Anthony, Andrew, Ruth
Hasenberg, Erich and Kathleen, Irene
Hazelton, Donald and Kathleen, Jane
Homann, Günther
Jones, Lloyd
Jory, Charles and Edna, Judith
Kaiser, Otto
Kaiser, Rose, Elisabeth, Rose Marie, Leonhard, Sara,
    Paul Gerhard
Keiderling, Karl and Irmgard, Roland, Peter, Ulrich, Esther,
    Agnes, Karl, Irmgard, Daniel
Keller, Kaspar
Klüver, Wilhelm and Lotte, Thomas, Christel, Konrad, Renatus,
    Anna
Laackmann, Martin and Alice
Lerchy, Julia
Löber, Christian and Sophie, Bärbel, Christian, Katharina,
    Joachim
Marchant, Will and Kathleen, Michael, Allister, Jeremy, Stephen
Martin, Arno and Ruth, Hanna, Hans, Ruth, Olga
Mercoucheff, Constantin
Mercoucheff, George
Moonje, Nadine

Pacey, Winifred
Pavitt, Leonard
Ridley, Thomas and Anita, Constance
Schulz, Lene
Sondheimer, Friedel
Sorgius, Herbert and Else, Elisabeth, Hans
Stängl, Josef and Ivy
Sumner, Bruce and Luise, Ursula, Anne
Trapnell, Brian and Nancy, Peter
Trümpi, Balz and Monika, Annemone, Eberhard
Vigar, George and Gertie, Eve, Michael, Godfrey
Walker, Sylvia, Clare
Watkins, Elizabeth

FEBRUARY 14, 1941

11 on the Andalucia Star

Mathis, Peter and Anni, Christoph, Peter, Jörg, Fida, Giovanni
Mathis, Margarita (Nona)
Rabbitts, Phyllis
Sondheimer, Elkan and Gertrud

MARCH 20, 1941

12 on the Empire Star

Ahrend, Ulrike
Britts, Philip and Joan
Catton, Fred
Cavanna, Paul
Crawley, Victor and Hilda
Headland, Robert and Dorothy
Patrick, Bill and Maria
Streatfeild, Kate

APRIL 23, 1941

63 on the Avila Star

    Ahrend, Lotti

    Arnold, Heini and Annemarie, Roswith, Christoph

    Barron, Dorothy, Constance

    Barron, Leslie

    Boller, Ursula

    Brown, John Ridley

    Caine, Chris, David

    Cassell, Ruth

    Catton, Nancy

    Cavanna, Peter

    Cocksedge, Edmund and Amy, Ian

    Eckardt, Marie

    Elston, Jack

    Evans, Gwynn and Buddug

    Gardner, Bill

    Greenslade, Dennis

    Hindley, Sydney and Marjorie

    Hüssy, Walter and Trudi, Franz, Bastel, David

    Illingworth, Walter

    Kiefer, Ria

    Lacey, Reginald

    Land, Edward

    Magee, Harry

    Mason, Arnold and Gladys, Jonathan, Rachel, David, Janet

    Myers, Milton

    Parker-Gray, Marjorie

    Robinson, John and Betty

    Savoldelli, Margot

    Simonds, Joy

    Stern, Margaret

    Wingard, Nils and Dora, Ingmar

    Winter, John

    Wright, Wilfred and Nina

Youle, Edna

Zumpe, Hans and Emy-Margaret, Heidi, Ben, Elisabeth, Burgel, Kilian

JULY 10, 1941
2 on the Andalucia Star

Phillips, Eric

Robertshaw, Bernard

SEPTEMBER 13, 1941
3 on a Houlder Brothers Line steamer

Caine, Norah, Robin

Davis, May

APPENDIX 2

Men, women, and children who died in Primavera,
1940–1961

Daniel Keiderling *(August 9, 1940 – March 30, 1941)*

Giovanni Mathis *(August 7, 1940 – April 8, 1941)*

Christine Kleiner *(December 24, 1939 – June 25, 1941)*

Felix Dreher *(October 25, 1940 – October 14, 1941)*

Christopher Sumner *(July 2, 1941 – November 2, 1941)*

Maria Trümpi *(January 8, 1942)*

Emmi-Christa Kleiner *(July 10, 1941 – May 5, 1942)*

Edith Arnold *(June 13, 1910 – April 3, 1943)*

Elisabeth Trümpi *(January 4, 1943 – August 9, 1943)*

Matthew Goodwin *(September 12, 1941 – August 18, 1943)*

André Allain *(November 6, 1940 – November 30, 1943)*

Mathis, daughter of Peter and Anni *(December 31, 1943)*

Angelika Martin *(May 18, 1944)*

Eunice Vigar *(August 9, 1943 – July 21, 1944)*

Marcella Stängl *(April 13, 1944 – January 24, 1946)*

Marianne Arnold *(July 24, 1947 – July 25, 1947)*

Fritz Kleiner *(February 25, 1905 – December 3, 1947)*

Albert Luis D'Hoedt *(December 29, 1947 – January 5, 1948)*

Adolf Braun *(August 6, 1893 – October 10, 1948)*

Philip Britts *(April 24, 1917 – January 31, 1949)*

Gottlieb Fischer *(March 14, 1949)*

Hermann Zotter *(March 28, 1874 – March 23, 1949)*

Maria Meier *(April 16, 1949)*

Jan Peter Fros *(January 4, 1941 – August 23, 1949)*

Trautel Dreher *(July 19, 1907 – August 5, 1950)*

Angela Vigar *(August 12, 1950)*

Ludwig Kleine *(April 13, 1875 – November 13, 1950)*

Fros, son of Hermann and Iet *(November 10, 1951)*

John Ridley Brown *(March 12, 1920 – November 12, 1951)*

Maria Else Loewenthal *(April 1, 1952 – June 16, 1952)*

Maria Chatterton *(April 29, 1948 – August 4, 1953)*

Margarita "Nona" Mathis *(April 16, 1875 – June 21, 1954)*

Augustin Thomann *(August 18, 1883 – December 1, 1954)*

Katharina "Käthe" Arnold *(March 30, 1884 – June 6, 1956)*

Alvin Barron *(February 22, 1957)*

Günther Homann *(September 27, 1911 – September 6, 1957)*

Wouter Fros *(April 4, 1948 – January 21, 1958)*

Rachel Marsden *(March 28, 1949 – August 27, 1958)*

Hermann J. W. Fros *(Nov. 20, 1958 – Nov. 24, 1958)*

Franz Kraupel *(1887 – June 18, 1960)*

Dolores Loewenthal *(February 5, 1961)*

Elsbeth Friedrich *(November 26, 1873 – July 31, 1961)*

Jens Mogensen *(April 13, 1890 – August 6, 1961)*

APPENDIX 3

Mennonite Peace Declaration

IN LATE JUNE 1936, some four hundred Dutch and German Mennonites, and a small handful of Americans, convened in Amsterdam for that year's Mennonite World Conference. Emmy Arnold and Hans Zumpe attended the conference as representatives of the Bruderhof, Emmy's recently deceased husband Eberhard having had several friends among the Dutch Mennonites.

Already suffering the fallout of Hitler's agenda (the Bruderhof had been spied on since 1933 and raided by the secret police; its school had been effectively shuttered; and most of its young men had had to flee the country to escape imprisonment for their refusal to join the German army) Emmy and Hans hoped to find kindred spirits. Instead, they discovered that no German Mennonite congregation was ready to stand up against the Nazis – at least not with regard to military service. In fact, an agreement had been made before the conference to speak about everything except "politics," which ruled out any frank discussion of the obligation of a Christian in relation to the state and the bearing of arms. In a report on the conference, the German Mennonite Christian Neff observed:

> Hans Zumpe…cast a light on the Bruderhof's attitude: renunciation of the world as a timely challenge based on early Anabaptist principles. Brother Dyck…represented the attitude of the German Mennonites, who, along with all sincere Christians, long for peace among the nations, but will still

obey their government – also by serving in the military – and will not lag behind their fellow Germans in their readiness for sacrifice. [11]

Not surprisingly, the conference as a whole was disappointing for the Bruderhof representatives. A smaller meeting after it, however, proved to be a highlight for Hans and Emmy and to have profound significance for the future of the Bruderhof. On July 4, at Fredeshiem, the Dutch Mennonite Jacob ter Meulen, a friend of Eberhard Arnold, led a delegation in addressing the "political" issues so carefully avoided at the larger conference that had just concluded. By the end of the day the group, which included all of the American Mennonite representatives, several Dutch Mennonites, a Pole, a German, and the two representatives of the Bruderhof, had issued the following joint statement:

Mennonite Peace Declaration

We, the undersigned Mennonites: groups, organizations, and individuals from all over the earth

• trusting in the Gospel of Jesus Christ, which calls people to serve the cause of peace and to fight the sin of war

• and convinced that the horrible means and measures of war now being readied in a constantly growing stream by all nations will be judged by God

• challenge the world's Mennonites to fulfill the task entrusted to us by God through the history of our Mennonite forebears, which is the proclamation of the gospel of peace.

We therefore turn to all brothers and sisters in the hope that they will, in every congregation, vigorously witness to our principle of peace and proclaim to the world our readiness for service in the spirit of Christ. We desire to work together so that we might realize this service of love in deed and render spiritual and material help to all those of our brothers who carry the conviction that God has called them to refuse military service, or who might have to suffer on account of their stand for peace.

L. D. G. Knipscheer	P. C. Hiebert	W. Mesdag
Frits Kuiper	Orie O. Miller	J. C. Dirkmaat
Harold S. Bender	P. R. Schroeder	Jan Gleysteen
Hans Zumpe	David Toews	C. Henry Smith
C. F. Klassen	Emmy Arnold	T. O. Hylkema
D. Attema	H. Brouwer	J. M. Leendertz
ter Meulen	Richard Nickel	

THIS REMARKABLE post-conference meeting received enthusiastic coverage in the American Mennonite press, but was not mentioned in the German *Mennonitische Blätter*. Still, the personal contacts forged and renewed during it proved of crucial importance to the Bruderhof. Two months later, in September 1936, Jacob ter Meulen visited Silum, the Bruderhof's temporary refuge in Liechtenstein, and in 1937, he helped arrange lodging for German Bruderhof members as they fled over the border into Holland. Meeting Harold S. Bender and Orie O. Miller, both leaders of the Mennonite Central Committee in the United States, proved to be equally important. Bender, who had visited the Rhön Bruderhof in 1930, kept abreast of the deteriorating situation of the community under the Nazis and did his best to provide practical help from across the ocean.

And in 1940, as the Bruderhof (now in exile in England) sought to leave the Old World altogether, it was Miller who helped facilitate the community's emigration to Paraguay.

1936

Chairman:
Vorsitzender:

HAROLD S. BENDER
Goshen,
Indiana U.S.A.

Secretary-Treasurer:
Geschäftsführer-Schatzmeister:

JACOB TER MEULEN,
Borneostraat 24
The Hague (Holland)
Den Haag
Tel. 551503 - Postgiro 83585

INTERNATIONAL MENNONITE PEACE COMMITTEE
INTERNATIONALES MENNONITISCHES FRIEDENSKOMITEE

FRIEDENSBEKENNTNIS DER MENNONITEN

Wir, die unterzeichneten Mennoniten: Gruppen, Organisationen und Einzelpersonen aus der ganzen Welt,

im Glauben an das Evangelium Jesu Christi, welches die Menschen zum Dienste am Frieden und zum Kampfe gegen die Sünde des Krieges aufruft,

und in der Ueberzeugung, dass die greulichen Kriegsmittel und Kriegsmassnahmen, die nunmehr in einem stetig wachsenden Strome von allen Völkern vorbereitet werden, von Gott gerichtet werden sollen,

fordern sämtliche Mennoniten der Welt auf, die Aufgabe zu erfüllen, mit der Gott uns in der Geschichte der Mennoniten, unserer Vorfahren, betraut hat und die in der Verkündigung des Friedensevangeliums besteht.

Wir wenden uns daher an alle Brüder und Schwestern mit dem Anliegen, in unseren Gemeinden überall von unsrem Friedensgrundsatz energisch Zeugnis abzulegen und in der Welt unsere Bereitschaft auszusprechen im Geiste Christi zu dienen. Wir wollen zusammen arbeiten, damit wir diesen Liebensdienst verwirklichen und damit wir all unseren Brüdern, die die Ueberzeugung in sich tragen, dass Gott sie dazu berufen hat den Militärdienst zu verweigern, oder die genötigt sein sollten wegen ihrer Friedensgesinnung zu leiden, geistige und materielle Hilfe leisten können.

L. D. G. Knipscheer	P. C. Hiebert	W. Mesdag
Frits Kuiper	Orie O. Miller	J. C. Dirkmaat
Harold S. Bender	P. R. Schroeder	Jan Gleysteen
Hans Zumpe	David Toews	C. Henry Smith
C. F. Klassen	Emmy Arnold	T. O. Hylkema
D. Attema	H. Brouwer	J. M. Leendertz
ter Meulen	Richard Nickel	

ENDNOTES

[1] Orie Miller to Jacob Siemens, September 28, 1940, in IX-6-3, Mennonite Central Committee, C.P.S., and other Corr., 1940–45, File 2, Mennonite Church USA Archives, Goshen, Indiana.

[2] Julius Legiehn to MCC, January 4, 1941, in IX-6-3, Mennonite Central Committee, C.P.S., and other Corr., 1940–45, File 4, Mennonite Church USA Archives, Goshen, Indiana.

[3] "Die Hutterischen sind da!" *Menno-Blatt*, January 1941.

[4] John D. Thiesen, *Mennonite & Nazi? Attitudes Among Mennonite Colonists in Latin America, 1933–1945* (Kitchener, Ontario: Pandora Press, 1999), 73.

[5] Thiesen, 102.

[6] Story of Fritz and Margarete Kliewer taken from Peter Klassen, *Frauenschicksale: Mennonitische Frauen auf der Wanderung, Flucht und Ansiedlung* (Uchte, Germany: Sonnentau Verlag, 2004), 121–168.

[7] Klassen, 160.

[8] Unpublished meeting transcript, Filadelfia Archives.

[9] Nicolai Siemens an die Brüder in Nord Amerika, April 4, 1941, Filadelfia Archives.

[10] Julius Legiehn to MCC, March 22, 1941, in IX-6-3, Mennonite Central Committee, C.P.S., and other Corr., 1940–45, File 4, Mennonite Church USA Archives, Goshen, Indiana.

[11] Christian Neff report, Verlag Heinrich Schneider, Karlsruhe, 1936, 43.

FOR FURTHER READING

THE BRUDERHOF IN PARAGUAY

Burn, Maureen. *Outcast But Not Forsaken* (1986). True stories from a Paraguayan leper colony reflect the wisdom of the Gospel in simple anecdotes and heartfelt reflections.

Dreher, Trautel. *The Stars Shall Light Your Journey* (1986). A war refugee from Europe, Dreher lost a son shortly after fleeing to Paraguay. This is her moving account of his brief life.

Wagoner, Bob and Shirley. *Community in Paraguay* (1991). Detailed letters home from an American couple who spent a year at Primavera, the Bruderhof's largest community from 1940 to 1961.

HISTORY OF THE BRUDERHOF

Arnold, Emmy. *A Joyful Pilgrimage* (1999). The autobiography of a woman whose spiritual quest led her from middle-class comfort to poverty and persecution.

Arnold, Annemarie. *Youth Movement to Bruderhof* (1986). Letters and dairy excerpts reveal a young woman's search for truth and paint a vivid picture of the youth movement that swept Germany after World War I.

Baum, Markus. *Against the Wind* (2002). The life of Eberhard Arnold, a Christian revolutionary known as the founder of the Bruderhof, as told by a radio journalist.

Mommsen, Peter. *Homage to a Broken Man* (2004). The dramatic life story of J. Heinrich Arnold and the community he guided until his death in 1982.

Mow, Merrill. *Torches Rekindled* (1989, 1990). A chronicle of the Bruderhof's history – "warts and all" – from the 1930s through the 1970s, by one of its members.

Klassen, Peter P. *Frauenschicksale: Mennonitische Frauen auf der Wanderung, Flucht und Ansiedlung* (2004). Stories of eight Mennonite women and the hardships they endured during the early years of settling Paraguay.

Stoesz, Edgar, and Stackley, Muriel T. *Garden in the Wilderness: Mennonite Communities in the Paraguayan Chaco, 1927–1997* (1999). An account of the development of Mennonite colonies in the Chaco, from their difficult early beginnings to their flourishing present.

Thiesen, John D. *Mennonite & Nazi? Attitudes Among Mennonite Colonists in Latin America, 1933–1945* (1999). Careful research on the sensitive topic of how Latin American Mennonites responded to National Socialism, by a scholar at Bethel College.

CHRISTIAN COMMUNITY

Arnold, Eberhard. *Selected Writings* (2000). Essential readings on following Christ in community – and in the world – from Orbis's acclaimed "Modern Spiritual Masters" series.

Arnold, Eberhard. *Why We Live in Community* (1995). A classic manifesto on Christian community, with two interpretive talks by Thomas Merton.

Arnold, Johann Heinrich. *Discipleship* (1994). Pithy excerpts on following Christ "in the daily grind" cover a wide variety of topics, from temptation to prayer, and from marriage to social justice.

Though some of these titles are out of print, most are available through online booksellers. Several can also be downloaded at www.plough.com *or* www.ploughbooks.co.uk.